L. A. Alderman

Centennial souvenir of Marietta, Ohio

Settled April seventh, 1788, celebration, April seventh, 1888

L. A. Alderman

Centennial souvenir of Marietta, Ohio
Settled April seventh, 1788, celebration, April seventh, 1888

ISBN/EAN: 9783743328198

Manufactured in Europe, USA, Canada, Australia, Japa

Cover: Foto ©ninafisch / pixelio.de

Manufactured and distributed by brebook publishing software (www.brebook.com)

L. A. Alderman

Centennial souvenir of Marietta, Ohio

Centennial Souvenir

OF

MARIETTA, OHIO

SETTLED APRIL SEVENTH, 1788

CELEBRATION,

APRIL SEVENTH, 1888.

[ALDERMAN]

It is to commemorate the first settlement, not of Marietta, not of Ohio, even, but of the great North West.—*Dr. I. W. Andrews.*

MARIETTA, O.
E. R. ALDERMAN & SONS, PRINTERS
[1887]

Copyrighted February, 1887, In the Office of the Librarian of Congress, Washington, D. C., by Mrs. L. A. Alderman.

All rights reserved.

This volume is merely a hand-book for hasty readers. The contents are culled from history already written. References have been made, chiefly, to Dr. S. P. Hildreth's works and the writings of Dr. I. W. Andrews. Five of the illustrations are reproductions in part from plates in Hildreth's Pioneer History. The outline, of what is often termed "romance in reality," of the story of the Blennerhassetts is much more closely allied to the early history of Marietta than is herein portrayed. Blennerhassett Papers, by W. H. Safford, are very complete upon this subject.

No attempt is made in biography, hence the absence of much, that might be said, in reference to the characteristic traits of the early settlers of Ohio, the founders of the State. L. A. A.

HERE, where but late a dreary forest spread,
Putnam, a little band of settlers led.
And now behold, with patriot joy elate
The infant settlement become a state;
See fruitful orchards and rich fields of grain,
See towns and cities rising on the plain,
While fair Ohio bears, with conscious pride,
New laden vessels to the ocean's tide.
                    [Harris' Journal, 1803.]

Illustrations:

Junction of Ohio and Muskingum rivers and partial view of Marietta and Harmar.
Map of Ohio Company's purchase.
Map of Northwest Territory.
Fort Harmar 1785.
Campus Martius 1791.
Marietta in 1792.
Farmer's Castle, Belpre.
Robinson's Mill, 1875.
Blennerhassett Mansion.
Mound at Marietta.
Ancient Earth-works.

The First Settlement
OF THE
NORTHWEST TERRITORY
MARIETTA OHIO
APRIL 7, 1788.

NESTLED among the foot-hills of mountains whose summits are less than one hundred miles away, and hemmed in, in happy seclusion, by two rivers, is a country town of historic name and fame. Half hidden by these hills, it is dreamily sleeping mayhap on the banks of the streams, the Ohio and Muskingum rivers. The former winds its way, in and out, between the hills of West Virginia and Ohio in a manner truly picturesque. The latter, after searching in many directions, for a pathway to the sea, greets the Ohio here, and ever after joins in silent communion with its waters. The town, Marietta, effeminate in name, being an abbreviation of Marie Antoinette, stands the peer of all other cities so called, this name being selected in honor of the Queen of France, in acknowledgment for her friendly and courteous manner towards Dr. Franklin, at that time Minister to France, representing the United states at the Court of Louis XVI. When she received the intelligence of this and the purport of the message was fully understood, she ordered, in recognition of the name, a bell, to be sent to the new settlement, for a public building. The bell never reached its destination, having been lost at sea, though there has long ing the certificates, for lands in the Ohio country—the Western Empire. In January, 1786, after a midnight conference, at Rutland, Mass., two gentlemen, Rufus Putnam and Benjamin Tupper, Generals in the American Army, issued a call, styled "Information," asking citizens to meet at places named, to elect delegates, to meet the first of March, in Boston, at the "Bunch of Grapes Tavern," there to form a company, the object of which was "to raise a fund for the sole purpose, and to be appropriated to the entire use of purchasing lands in the Western Territory for the benefit of the company."

The citizens of several counties met and elected their delegates in pursuance to this call. At this meeting, after a deliberate discussion of two or three days, an orpanization was perfected, after which they adjourned to meet again in one year; but with the understanding that they immediately set to work to raise funds for the purchase of lands, by selling shares, each share to represent one thousand dollars in certificates, and ten dollars in gold to be paid by each share-holder for defraying expenses soon to accrue. The first call was to citizens of Massachusetts, but many from other states were willing to take shares, provided a colony could be established on lands intact. At a second meeting, March 1, 1787, at Bracket's Tavern, Boston, it was shown that two hundred and fifty shares had been disposed of, which was deemed sufficient for further proceedings. A committee of five were selected to draft a plan for the approbation of the convention. These were Messrs. Putnam, Cutler, Brooks, Sargent, and Cushing. The company thus formed was known as the "Ohio Company of Associates." Winthrop Sargent was clerk of these meetings. This Association is known at present as the Ohio Company.

By this time Massachusetts, Connecticut, and Virginia had ceded their territory back to the United States, with exceptions of small reservations; but treaties with the Indians were still unsettled. The circumstances were such that it was deemed advisable to urge the immediate action of Congress, then in session in New York City, to allow the purchase of lands for the Company. The gentlemen appointed to confer with Congress were General Rufus Putnam, Gen. Samuel H. Parsons and Rev. Manasseh Cutler, with Major Winthrop Sargent as Secretary. To these were afterwards added General James M. Varnum, of Rhode Island, and Richard Platt, of New York, as Treasurer. Their first agent to visit New York was Gen. Samuel H. Parsons. The Congress then in session had under consideration the laws that were to govern the territory of which this purchase was to be a small portion. They adjourned without any action in regard to the purchase by the Company, and did not meet again until in July, when Dr. Cutler visited New York, and went directly before the commissioners with his requests and was successful in a short time in contracting for one and a half million acres at two-thirds of a dollar per acre; the final contract, however, closed for something over nine hundred and sixty-four thousand acres, represented by eight hundred and seventeen shares. The contract was signed by Samuel Osgood and Arthur Lee, on behalf of the Board of the Treasury of the United States, and by Manasseh Cutler and Winthrop Sargent for the Ohio Company. It will be noticed that the famous Ordinance of July 13th, 1787, was passed simultaneously with this purchase of lands by the Company.

The contract for the purchase was, however, not finally concluded until in October, 1787. In November of that year the Ohio Company decided to send, at its own expense, a number of men, members of the Company, to their new purchase, expecting them to prepare the way for others who were soon to follow with their families. To assist these were surveyors, carpenters, boat-builders, and men for all kinds of work. They assembled at two places. A part of them, under the management of Major Haffield White, met at Danvers, Massa chusetts, and others, with General Rufus Putnam as superintendent, at Hartford, Connecticut.

Those who met at Danvers came first over the mountains, through the wilderness, toward the Western Empire. The early part of the year 1788 was spent at Sumrill's Ferry, in the wilds of Pennsylvania, building the boats that were to carry them to their destination. They were joined by General Putnam and his men, and left their winter quarters April 2, landing at Marietta—which was then designated as "The country on the banks of the Ohio and Muskingum,"—

APRIL SEVENTH, 1788.

Below are the names of these Pioneers, the first settlers of the Northwest Territory:

GENERAL RUFUS PUTNAM, Superintendent of the Settlement and Surveys,
COLONEL EBENEZER SPROAT,
COLONEL RETURN J. MEIGS,
MAJOR ANSELM TUPPER,
JOHN MATHEWS, Surveyor,
MAJOR HAFFIELD WHITE, Steward and Quartermaster,
CAPTAIN JONATHAN DEVOL,
CAPTAIN JOSIAH MUNRO,
CAPTAIN DANIEL DAVIS,
CAPTAIN JETHRO PUTNAM,
CAPTAIN WILLIAM GRAY,
PEREGRINE FOSTER, ESQ.,
SAMUEL CUSHING,
ISAAC DODGE,
ISRAEL DANTON,
EARL SPROAT,
ALLEN DEVOL,
WILLIAM MASON,
EDMOND MOULTON,
BENJAMIN SHAW,
EZEKIEL COOPER,
JARVIS CUTLER,
OLIVER DODGE,
SAMUEL FELSHAW,
HEZEKIAH FLINT, JR.,
JOSIAH WHITRIDGE,
BENJAMIN GRISWOLD,
THEOPHILUS LEONARD,
WILLIAM MILLER,
DANIEL BUSHNELL,
PHINEAS COBURN,

Hesekiah Flint,
Amos Porter, Jr.,
John Gardner,
Elizar Kirtland,
Joseph Lincoln,
Jabez Barlow,
Ebenezer Cory,
Allen Putnam,
Joseph Wells,

David Wallis,
Gilbert Devol, Jr.,
Jonas Davis,
Josiah White,
Henry Maxon,
William Moulton,
Simeon Martin,
Peletiah White.

There were forty-eight of the Pioneers, Return J. Meigs arriving the 12th of April. The last meeting of the share-holders of the Ohio Company was held in Massachusetts in March, 1788. They adjourned to meet on the lands of the Company in July of that year, which they designated as "the settlement on the Ohio and Muskingum rivers," they not then knowing it by the name, Adelphi, as the settlement was first called by the Pioneers. (The Marietta College Library possesses the original contract for the purchase by the Company—or rather by the agents.) It is hoped, that by this detail of the preparation for the settlement at Marietta, to instill into the minds of the younger readers the important fact that the events herein outlined are worthy a careful investigation which may precede or follow the celebration now contemplated. Carefully consider these long and continued transactions that at last secured such glorious results. May the memory of the men who participated in them be ever cherished by all the generations that follow.

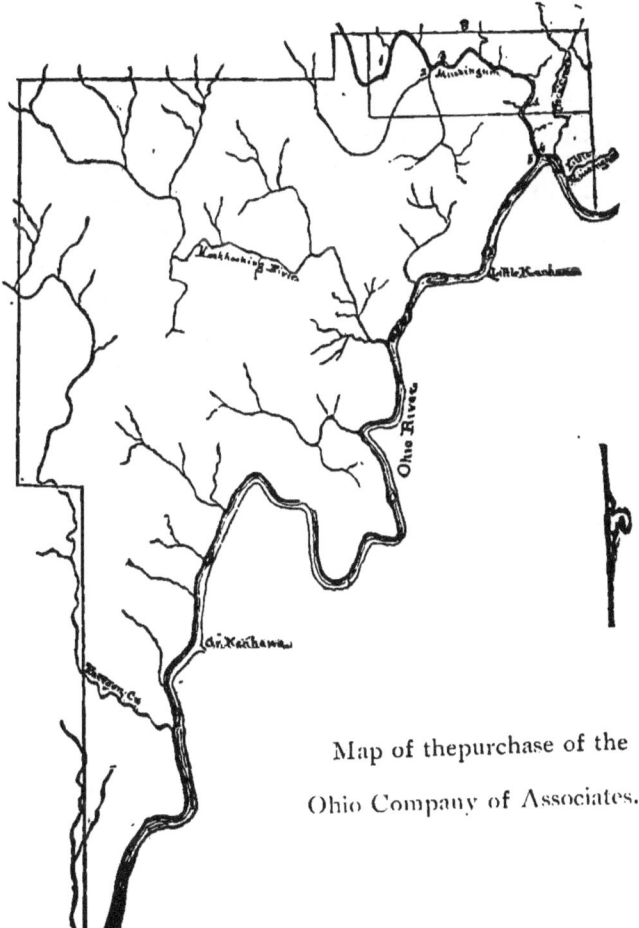

Map of the purchase of the Ohio Company of Associates.

The Ordinance of 1787.

As one seems a compact or part of the other, so it is proper to follow with a brief allusion to this ordinance.

It has been truthfully said, that this Ordinance would never have existed but for the formation of the Ohio Company, or gentlemen representing it before the Colonial Congress then in session in New York city, and just as truly was it said that the final settlement of claims against the Government, by these share-holders in the company, "would not have been completed but for this Ordinance." This was a provisional government enacted for the Northwest Territory, governing first, the settlers of the Ohio Company, as they were in advance of all others. A hasty review will be made, in order to show the wisdom of the enactments, hoping it may lead to a more careful study of them by such as are interested in the laws yet governing that territory, or rather the States that have emanated from the territory, for which these laws were made.

First.—No person demeaning himself in a peaceable and orderly manner, should ever be molested on account of his mode of worship or religious sentiments in said Territory.

Second.—This article provided for the benefits of *habeas corpus,* jury trial, and the fullest protection of the individual under a just government.

Third.—"Religion, morality and knowledge being necessary to good government and the happiness of mankind, schools and the means of education shall forever be encouraged." This article also asks for good will towards the Indians; advises not going to war with them, only as it is sanctioned by Congress; and laws are promised founded upon the principles of justice and humanity, in order to govern peaceably if possible. To carry out this article properly, made

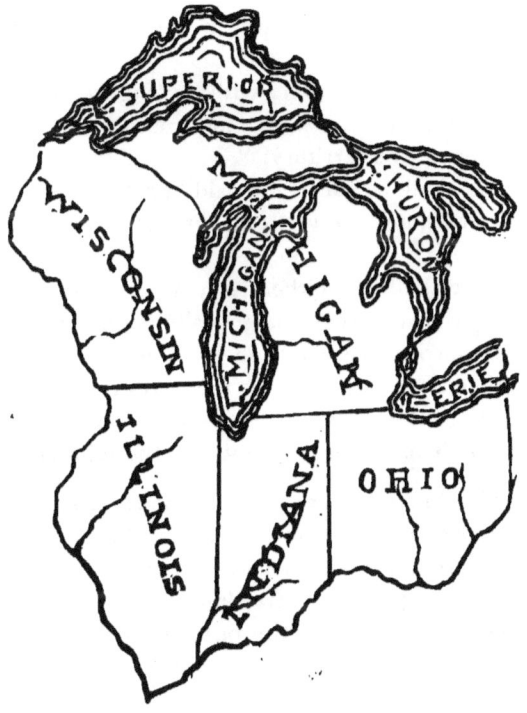

Map of the Northwest Territory.

the long delay in settling the Indian war from 1791 to 1795. More severe measures in the outset might have saved much suffering, anxiety and expense. The leniency of the government made it necessary for the settlers themselves to carry on the war at their own expense. They disbursed over fourteen thousand dollars, eleven thousand of which, according to excellent authority, was never refunded to them by the Government.

Fourth.—This article had to do with levying taxes for the support of the territorial and general government, also for the free use of all navigable streams of the territory.

Fifth.—There shall be formed in said territory not less than three nor more than five states, the western states to be bounded by the Mississippi river, &c.

Sixth.—"There shall be neither slavery nor involuntary servitude in the territory otherwise than the punishment of crime after conviction." The stigma of slavery was never to be placed upon the statutes governing the territory or of any of the states thereafter formed.

On the question of slavery, Mr. Lawton, who has descendants in Barlow, wrote in 1819, a poem, from which the following is an extract:

> "Confusion strange, to grasp in the same hand
> The blood-stained scourge, the peaceful olive wand.
> Hail Marietta, thou, my native town,
> I'll sing thy praise, for freedom there is known.
> No petty tyrants tread thy peaceful streets,
> No mourning slave the passing stranger meets;
> Blessed be thy name, while fair Ohio's waves,
> Shall part thy borders from a land of slaves.*
> May well-frought barges ever line thy shores
> And smiling plenty rest within thy doors."

---

*Virginia and Kentucky were then slave States.

That this Ordinance has been well tested the people of the United States can fully and earnestly substantiate. To the fact that it has proved an unqualified success for a century, they can readily attest. The fore-sight and wisdom shown, in the foregoing enactments, far exceeded the most sanguine expectations of the promoters of the laws. The commemorating of the ordinance, is then, an event for rejoicing. It became a law July 13, 1787, and soon thereafter the contract with the Government, by the Ohio Company, was made final, and measures were immediately taken for occupying their claims by the shareholders of the Company. It is plainly portrayed in the annals of history, that the participants in the adjustment of governmental affairs, after the close of the Revolutionary War, were men who proved themselves worthy of any trust. This has been further verified by the success and continued prosperity of the country opened to civilization, by their joint efforts, at that time.

The settlement at Marietta had many advantages; these settlers were men possessed of the best possible knowledge then attainable at the leading Eastern colleges, men versed in military tactics and trials of war, many of them being officers and soldiers of the Revolutionary war; men already disciplined for hardships and trials, men of great courage and fortitude, of marked intelligence and refinement.

They had been the means of assisting all in their power to thwart England's determined supremacy over them or their government, and in saving this territory to the possession of the United States. They had, in a measure, assisted in the formation of the laws that were to govern it. They showed themselves willing to purchase and accept a portion of it as their own and again to redeem it, by war with the Indians, carried on at a most inconvenient time—ever after to live in peace, as law-abiding citizens under the protection of such laws as they had reasons to fully understand.

The Mayflower.

In the cold wintry days of 1620 there lay at its moorings, on a rocky Massachusetts sea-coast, the Mayflower, that had brought the Puritans to their new home, the wilderness of America. Whipped by the waves and lashed by storms of the winter months, it looked a comfortless in the spring-time as the shores had been to the little Pilgrim band; there was little that was inviting on either ship or shore.

In trying to establish their colony these people had withstood hardships with a zeal and undaunted courage never equaled. The warmth of the sun in the spring days was wished for, looked for but came not. Their courage faltered, they questioned their judgment in choice, if choice it was, of location. They pondered upon their prospects, and wondered if this was to be the cold, bleak world they had so far found it.

An incident of unseeming moment took place which gave them renewed courage. The voice of Nature announced to them that the warm rays of the sun were already quickening to life the wild-flowers of the forest, and they hailed with delight the pale unassuming bloom of the Mayflower, or Trailing Arbutus, with its exquisite fragrance. Then they exclaimed "Our God is with us, He will not desert us."

Not altogether different was an occurrence nearly two hundred years later. After a winter of severe trials, fatiguing work and anxiety, there was set afloat, on a small stream at Sumrill's Ferry, in Pennsylvania, another boat, another Mayflower, accompanied by other smaller craft, whose destination was to a wilderness, "on the banks of the Ohio and Muskingum rivers," but to the occupants of this river craft, their destiny was not foretold; the veil of futurity hung heavily before them. With nothing of romance in their journey down the Ohio, they reached their new prospects with scarcely an incident recorded.

It was not long until the April sun shone out and revealed a scene not altogether desolate. To the observant eye, here, too, could be found the sweet, fragrant little Mayflower—Trailing Arbutus—breaking the crusty dead leaves and searching the sunlight, offering its quiet welcome to the few strangers who had come hither to prepare the way for many more. A little later on, the wild roses burst from their confinement and bade, in their way, these settlers a double welcome or greeting. All nature put on an air of gayety as if to dispel sober moments and scatter them, anywhere, never to be again remembered.

What was all this display of nature to men who had a heavy task before them, whose first thought was shelter from storms, and protection for the nights? These pleasant surroundings were trivial, indeed, to such mem, and the last to be recognized, perhaps, yet, their silent voice and influence were beneficial, for the tidings that went back to the homes in New England were: "We are greatly pleased with the prospect." These encouraging words reached the listening ears of those who were already active in their preparation for a journey to the new country.

After the first successful voyage of the Mayflower, boatmen returned many times to the "Ferry" to meet others who came thus far overland, and by them were transported to the new settlement. Once here the Pioneers were greeted with cheers, and welcomed to their new home in the wilderness.

It is accredited by some that, after the first salutes of welcome, by the soldiers at Fort Harmar, had died in faint echoes among the hills, and a tent had been pitched for General Putnam and his assistants, a code of laws were established and fastened upon the trunk of a tree for general reference.

As many of the men were officers and soldiers of the Continental Army, well versed in and accustomed to military discipline, this precaution for good conduct could readily be supported. No mention, however, is made of any such forethought until the 4th of July of that year. They then enacted laws—temporary, by resolutions—and these *were* "tacked up on the smooth bark of a beech tree." Governor St. Clair arrived the 9th of July, and had power, vested in authority from the Congress, of which he was President when he was appointed Governor of the Territory, to execute the laws enacted by that Congress, embodied in the Ordinauce of 1787, so that the temporary laws were not greatly needed. The town or settlement was called Adelphi until the arrival of St. Clair, when by formal resolution, the name was changed to Marietta.

The State of Ohio Founded.

The forests were felled, cabins erected and seed planted for the crops of the season. The two most important occupations were those of the surveyors, in the measurement of lands, and guards whose duty it was to give the alarm, when there were any suspicious signs, or presence of Indians. The Indians bade the Pioneers a hearty welcome, but afterwards proved very treacherous and unreliable, characteristics they ever possessed. These traits did not surprise General Putnam. He had noted treaties made and treatses broken, and also had observed that the Indians were not pleased to see the land cleared and houses built. He demanded a vigilant watch, and as soon as possible, ordered the erection of forts, block-houses and stockades, for the better protection of the settlers and their possessions.

One inducement for the settlers here was, that a military post had been already established at Fort Harmar. Another was the information from surveyors and map-makers, who had some knowledge of this section. They reported the valleys fertile, the hills abounding in mineral wealth, and that salt and coal were plentiful. There were negotiations pending for treaties with the Indians, but of the uncertainty of what the result might be, it was deemed best to build a fort, which was afterwards called Campius Martius—or military camp.

The Pioneers held in veneration and remembrance the first Fourth of July. The oration on that occasion was delivered by Gen. James M. Varnum, one of the Judges of the territory. The anniversary of their landing was commemorated by an address, given elsewhere. The address on the Fourth of July, 1788, was made by Return J. Meigs, Jr. It has too much of the ideal to be in harmony with the tenor of these notes, but this gentleman was ever hopeful and cheerful. The lines were composed one hundred years ago, so let them be recorded here. The address was a poem but only an extract is preserved:

> Enough of tributary praise is paid
> To virtue living or to merit, dead;
> To happier themes the rural muse invites
> To calmest pleasures, and serene delights.
> To us glad fancy, brightest prospect shows,
> Rejoicing nature all around us glows;
> Here, late the savage hid, in ambush lay,
> Or roamed the uncultured valleys for his prey;
> Here, frowned the forest, with terrific shade
> No cultured fields exposed, no opening glade.
> How changed the scene! see nature clothed in smiles
> With joy repays the laborer for his toils.
> Her hardy gifts rough industry extends,
> The groves bow down, the lofty forest bends.
> On every side the cleaving ax is found,
> The oak and tall beach thunder to the ground:
> And see the spires of MARIETTA rise,

And domes and temples swell into the skies;
Here, justice reigns, and foul dissensions cease,
Her walks be pleasant and her paths be peace.
Here, swift Muskingum rolls its rapid waves,
There, fruitful valleys fair Ohio laves;
On its smooth surface gentle zephyrs play,
The sunbeams tremble with a placid ray.
What future harvests on its bosom glide,
And loads of commerce swell the downward tide,
Where Mississippi joins in length'ning sweep
And rolls majestic to the Atlantic deep.
Along these banks see distant villas spread;
Here, waves the corn, and there extends the mead,
Here, find the murmur of the gurgling rills,
There, bleat the flocks upon a thousand hills.
Fair opes the lawn,—the fertile fields extend,
The kindly showers, from smiling heaven descend;
The skies drop fatness on the blooming vale
From spicy shrubs ambrosial sweets exhale,
Fresh fragrance rises from the flow'rets bloom
And ripening vineyards breathe a glad perfume.
Gay swell the music of the warbling grove
And all around is melody and love.
Here, may religion fix her blest abode,
Bright emanation of creative God;
Here, charity extends her liberal hand,
And mild benevolence o'er-spread the land.
In harmony and social virtues blend
Joy without measure, rapture without end.

[Harris's Tour, 1803.]

War with the Indians.

In 1791, there was an unqualified out-break among the Indians, so that as each new settlement was formed, each had to have its local protection, and sufficient force within itself to guard its own garrisons. The settlements at Belpre, at Waterford, at Wolf Creek Mills, and at Big Bottom, thirty miles up the Muskingum, were all protected by small defenses. There, though they had a Block-house, the inmates were taken by surprise, and the settlement entirely destroyed by the killing of the people and the burning of their houses.

During the years of the Indian war from 1791 to 1795, there was great suffering and privation; the hardships were multiplied by lack of provisions, and money to buy with. There were not men sufficient to provide for the necessary wants and at the same time carry on a war with a desperate enemy, at their own expense. When the war began 246 of the 287 able bodied men of the settlements were enlisted to defend the different neighborhoods, leaving only 41 not on duty. The war, at the same time kept many from coming who had expected to join the Ohio Company here.

The merchandise from eastern cities was secured with great difficulty, there being no specie as a basis of currency. Eastern cities established a greatly reduced rate of value on the final certificates, that the soldiers had accepted as their pay for services in the War of the Revolution. They had for local traffic orders or vouchers for military duty in defense of the garrisons, which served for small transactions. These orders, redeemable by the treasury of the Company in Philadelphia, were all paid at their face value, and served the place of gold and silver.

Supplies were brought to the upper Ohio on horse-back or in wagons, and then carried in boats down the river. Small dug-outs or canoes were first used, then keel-boats and barges, which increased in size and numbers as the traffic increased, some of these being sixty feet long, and from twelve to eighteen feet wide, covered sometimes with canvass, and called "arks." Many of these barges were simply but strongly built and fastened with wooden pins, so they were easily taken apart and used in the construction of buildings.

Monopolies were not tolerated in the early history of this country. After a part of the territory was organized as a state, the townships of land where salt springs were known to exist, were reserved by the State, also certain lands on the Muskingum. The reason given for this action being: "Had such property become the property of an individual he would have had it in his power to create a monopoly of this article and been able to oppress a great portion of the citizens of the State." Salt was so scarce in early times at Marietta that merchants sent men with ox-teams to the Scioto country to procure this article. The journey often occupied a month or more until the return. The salt sold rapidly for six and seven dollars per bushel, and was in great demand; there was a bountiful supply of wild meat, the buffalo, bear, deer and other wild game, with wild turkeys so plentiful that they sold for twelve and one-half cents each, and the streams were swarming with fish. The journeys to salt springs in the Miami country were suspended during the war. It was also hazardous to hunt the wild game, or fish in the streams. The scarcity of gold and silver made it difficult to procure their equivalent in provisions, so every form of traffic was carried on to procure food, and children cried for this, which at times could not be provided for them. Sickness followed famine, carrying off many. The millions now enjoying their happy homes ought ever to be mindful of the purchase price of their privileges, by the early settlers of the country. Have the memories of the trials of the Pioneers out run their limits? By no means.

The sentiment and appreciation of the value of their wise provisions, grow with the years.

Fort Harmar.

Defenses of the Frontier.

On the west bank of the Muskingum, at its confluence with the Ohio river, once stood a fort, erected for the protection of the frontier. It was hoped, by this precaution, to encourage immigration. This was one inducement for the Ohio Company to select lands at this place, though but a small body of troops were ever stationed here at any one time. It afforded some protection, for the only other military post at that time along the Ohio river was Fort McIntosh, thirty miles below Pittsburg.

Fort Harmar was built by a detachment of Government troops, in 1785, under the command of Major Doughty, and named for the colonel of his regiment.

The spot for the fort was well chosen, as an excellent view was obtained from the upper out-looks of the towers. The rivers could be seen for many miles in either direction, up or down the streams.

The guns were small, mounted on wheels, and served oftener for giving a salute than for repelling an attack. They were sufficient to repulse an enemy whose weapons were bows and arrows or muskets.

Major Doughty was a man of excellent taste. He had the grounds surrounding the fort cleared of the forest trees. The grassy lawn was interspersed with beds of gaily blooming flowers, and well-kept walks. Back of the fort he had a fine peach orchard, from seeds of his own planting. The soldiers cared for the grounds, and were glad of the pastime, for with them time hung heavily. Aside from the frequent friendly visits of the Indians, and the negotiations for treaties, there was little to do, to engage their minds. They greeted the Pioneers with great enthusiasm, when they came, and as a treaty of peace was then under consideration between the Indians and the officers at the fort, quite a number of chiefs witnessed their arrival, Captain Pipe, of the Delawares, welcoming the whites to their hunting grounds.

But in their visits, a few weeks afterwards, the Indians were greatly displeased to see cabins built and crops planted, before the treaties with them had been settled.

At the out-break of the Indian war in 1791 the troops, so long stationed here, were withdrawn, for a post farther west, Fort Washington, and a much smaller number sent here in command of Captain Zeigler.

Many neighborly visits were exchanged between the occupants of the fort and the pioneers of the forest on the opposite side of the Muskingum. Some of the settlers occupied houses within the fort, others built in close proximity to it and relied upon its protection in time of attack by the Indians. About three-fourths of an acre of ground was inclosed within the walls, and a well, at that time in the center of the enclosure, has recently been located far down the river bank, the depth shallow. The frosts and floods have broken and washed the banks away so that a frontage that was once sufficient in size for a parade ground for a battalion of men has long since disappeared.

CAMPUS MARTIUS.

The Indians had frequently broken former treaties, and General Putnam at once decided to protect the settlers against future outbreaks. He advised the erection of a strong defense near the settlement, which was immediately begun, but not completed for three years. It was built at the expense of the Ohio Company and in part by individuals building houses within the walls, at their own personal expense, occupying them for some years as the Indian war made it a necessity.

Campus Martius was built upon ground with Washington street as a Southern boundary, and Second street the Eastern boundary, and fronting towards the Muskingum river; Hon. William P. Cutler's residence and grounds are near the site upon which Campus Martius stood.

This defense was three-fourths of a mile from the "Point," where the first houses were erected, and connected with it by a narrow, winding path through the forest, with substantial bridges crossing the streams, that still intersect the lower portion of the city.

Marietta in 1792.

Dr. S. P. Hildreth in 1848, in his Pioneer history, says: "All these tenements have long since passed away, like the people who dwelt within them, and their places are supplied with substantial brick buildings. It is nevertheless pleasant to look upon the likeness of what has been before our own times, and to dwell upon the remembrance of our hardy ancestors, who struggled long and manfully with famine, poverty, and the red men of the forest, to provide a home, not only for themselves, but for their children. *This little spot is the germ from whence sprung the State of Ohio, with its millions of inhabitants, and shall not its remembrance be preserved.*"

The Point in 1792 projected far out into the waters of the Ohio river on one side and the Muskingum on the other. The houses were in close proximity to each other and a small detachment of soldiers was sometimes stationed here, during the Indian war.

The Stockade, which included Campus Martius, with about forty acres of ground, is still so called by old residents. General Putnam's wisdom was clearly shown when it was found necessary to make haste in the completion of the garrison, and the immediate occupancy of it by the settlers. It proved a strong defense against the Indians during the war, and was considered by far the best defense of the frontier. The outer walls were two story log houses, joined compactly together, opening into an inner court, one hundred and forty feet square. Each angle of the fort was protected by a block-house and a tower, built still higher, for an out-look, so that the approach of Indians could be more clearly discerned and announced by an alarm from the guns, if needed. Aside from the many families here quartered, the government officers for the territory occupied buildings also. Governor St. Clair and his family resided in one of the corner buildings; Winthrop Sargent, Secretary, used the one directly over the door, or heavy gate, as an office. One was used for a store-house for supplies, another for church service, for holding court, or any gathering or entertainment of the settlers. In this same building the day schools were taught, and the first Sunday school, organized by Mary Lake. Here the American Union Lodge of Free Masons re-organized their lodge, after an adjournment of seven years. The first organization was among the officers and soldiers of the Revolutionary war which moved its place of meeting with the general orders of the army. The adjournment was in 1783, and the reorganization in 1790.

Much time and ingenuity was consumed in defense of this garrison. After Campus Martius was made secure within, the heavy gates placed on their hinges, the outer defenses were looked after. First, a heavy picket fence, leaning outward, was built around it and heavy gates hung at the openings. Beyond this, a high brush fence with the small twigs lying inward towards the fence. This proved a very formidable protection as the large limbs were sharpened and driven into the ground. There was but little loss of life among the settlers at Marietta in comparison with many other places in the State. Some of these were the result of carelessness for their own safety.

Some idea of the anxiety of the early settlers, in regard to attacks by the Indians, may be obtained from the following by Dr. S. P. Hildreth in regard to the military discipline kept up during the war:

"The garrison at Campus Martius was kept under the strictest discipline by order of Governor St. Clair. The men were divided into squads, and called out to their posts by daylight. The bastions were occupied every night by four of these squads. After dark the sentries were set, and the watch-word cried every half hour during the night. A magazine of ammunition was placed in the North-west block-house, in the upper loft, and long poles with iron spears, kept in each of the block-houses for the defense of the doors, should the Indians break through the inner rampart of palisades. A four-pound cannon was placed in each of the bastions of the north-east and south-west blockhouses to defend the approaches in these quarters, and especially to be fired as alarm guns, to give notice to the inhabitants, of danger, when out at work in the field. This strict discipline was kept up for about four years, or until after the victory of General Wayne."

The tribes of Indians in the Northwest Territory at the time of the settlement at Marietta, were Delawares, Mohawks, Wyandots, Shawanees and Senecas. The five nations with which treaties of peace were declared in January, 1789, at Fort Harmar, were the Chippewas, Ottawas, Miamis, Pottewatamies and Sacs. The treaty was made by Gov. St. Clair, they to relinquish all rights to the Northwest Territory, and to further carry out stipulations of a former treaty, that of October, 1784. After this treaty these tribes were invited to a grand feast in the hall of Campus Martius, then not completed.

A hundred acres of land was first offered by the Ohio Company to any able-bodied man who would settle upon their lands, permanently, and help in defense of the settlers until the close of the war.

A number from Virginia and Pennsylvania responded to the offer of this bounty of land. This was found to be impoverishing the Company so rapidly that the Directors appealed to Congress to relieve them of a part of their purchase. Their request was granted and one hundred thousand acres out of the original purchase donated by Congress to such settlers. With the exception of this and a few months' pay of the militia the Ohio Company bore all the expense of their defenses, for the different settlements in the purchase, and for all supplies necessary in carrying on the war. Many who accepted lands upon conditions of actual settlement sold out at low prices early after the close of the war and returned to their former homes, thus retarding the rapid settlement of the country as anticipated by the donation of lands.

The total expense incurred by the Company in money, for wages, rations, guards, scouts, ammunition, lumber and materials of whatever kind, including charges made by Rufus Putnam, Robert Oliver and Griffen Green for services, was $14,788.92; of this the United States paid $3,358.12; balance due the Company, $11,350.90.

Farmer's Castle, Belpre.

Belpre, twelve miles below Marietta, was protected by three defenses. The first being the most important, called Farmer's Castle.

This was built upon a high bank, about opposite where the excursion boats now land, at Blennerhassett Island. There was a commanding view of the Ohio river, an interminable swamp back of it. It must have appeared to good advantage from the river with the heavy wooded hills as a back-ground.

The settlement here was not unlike the one at Marietta. The garrison was under military discipline, and religious services and schools were at once established. Miss Bathsheba Rouse, of New Bedford, Massachusetts, taught in the summer season, and Daniel Mayo, of Boston, in the winter. The people were called together for services on Sabbath by the beating of a drum. Over two hundred men, women and children lived in Farmer's Castle, and in Goodale's and Stone's garrisons, two smaller defenses on either side of the "Castle," until the constant annoyance by the Indians ceased, and their lives seemed more secure.

Fort Freye.

This defense was named for Captain Joseph Freye, and built similarly to Campus Martius, except it was triangular in shape, with one side fronting on the Muskingum river. It was located just below Beverly, on the same side of the river. There was also a garrison at Plainfield—now Waterford—named Fort Tyler, for Dean Tyler, one of the Pioneers.

Not many lives were lost in this section, though the number killed by the Indians during the war was over fifteen hundred whites in the different settlements in what is now Ohio, and the torture of constant fear was great in this region.

Another and very important precaution taken by the settlers was to employ rangers, persons familiar with every portion of the country, as hunters, enlisted by Col. Ebenezer Sproat; they were to traverse the country many miles in all directions, hastening to camp to give the alarm if Indians were seen. There were four or six for each settlement. They dressed in a semi savage costume and adopted any disguise that would most successfully deceive the enemy. The first to scout for Campus Martius were Joseph Rogers and Edward Henderson, the former being killed, after one of their detours, when near the garrison.

TERRITORIAL GOVERNMENT.—ORGANIZATION OF COUNTIES AND STATE.

In July, 1788, Arthur St. Clair, Governor of the Territory, with his secretary, Winthrop Sargent, arrived at Marietta. These gentlemen, with the Judges, James M. Varnum, Samuel H. Parsons and John Cleve Symms, the first two already here, constituted the representatives of the Colonial Government for the Territory, with full power to adopt and execute such local laws as were deemed necessary. They were appointed to these offices at the time of the passage of the Ordinance of 1787. On the 15th of July, soon after his arrival, Governor St. Clair published the act of Congress giving him his commission as Governor. On the 26th of July a proclamation was issued creating the county of Washington. In August the land was surveyed into lots, and the village made the county seat of the first county in the Northwest Territory. This village, town, or settlement, included within its boundaries what is now Marietta township. It was not incorporated as a town until the year 1800, and did not have a Mayor until 1825. Harmar did not have an independent government by corporate act until 1837.

The first Territorial Legislature met in 1799, when Paul Fearing and Colonel R. J. Meigs were the representatives from Washington county. Colonel Robert Oliver was one of the five members of the upper house of this legislature, where he continued in office until the State was organized, in February, 1803. Ephraim Cutler and William R. Putnam represented this county in the second Territorial Legislature. The first Court in the territory was held in Campus Martius, September 2d, 1788. Colonel Ebenezer Sproat was sheriff. In referring to this, General Putnam says: "Happily for the credit of the people, there was no suit, either civil or criminal, brought before the Court."

Arthur St. Clair was Territorial Governor until the formation of the State, and its admission into the Union.

Edward Tiffin was the first governor of the State. William Henry Harrison was the first representative to Congress from Ohio as a State. From the landing of Rufus Putnam and his associates, fourteen years elapsed to the time when the act was passed admitting Ohio into the Union. The constitution was framed at Chillicothe between the first and twenty-ninth day of November, 1802. This constitution was not submitted to the people of the territory for their approval, but was sent directly to Congress. It was not acted upon until February 19th, 1803, when that body passed the act entitled "an act to provide for the due execution of the laws of the United States within the State of Ohio." By this act Ohio became a State. At the time of admission there were nine counties; eight others organized at the first session of the State Legislature, making seventeen at the time the State Seal was designed. This accounts, it is claimed, for the seventeen arrows on the seal.

WASHINGTON COUNTY.

This county has somewhat diminished in size since its first organization. When a part of the Northwest Territory, it included within its boundaries one-half of what is now the State of Ohio. Its present area is limited to a fraction over six hundred square miles, with a population of about fifty thousand inhabitants. The county seat—Marietta—and its immediate suburbs has a population of ten thousand. This section is a typical New England country, hilly, with water in abundance, streams in every portion of the county, which is interspersed at short distances with pleasant country villages. Along the Muskingum are the towns of Beverly, Waterford, Lowell and Harmar. On the Ohio, Newport, surveyed and laid off into town lots in 1797, and Belpre, the first settlement after Marietta; fourteen families going from Marietta to this locality. There are growing centers in the eastern part of the county, along the different lines of railroads. Macksburg and Elba in the oil district, and the villages of Watertown, Barlow, Vincent, Cutler and Bartlett in the western portion.

The land holders have generally tilled the soil for a competence, but more recently much attention has been given to the raising of stock, to which the lands of the county are admirably adapted.

As early as 1789, there were peach trees laden with fruit on grounds adjacent to Fort Harmar. In 1795, there were peach orchards at Belpre and large, well-bearing apple orchards in 1800. Washington county has always kept up a creditable reputation in the culture of fruit and is noted for its shipments of small fruits, strawberries, grapes, plums, peaches and large supplies of apples. Wool is an important and increasing export. Coal is abundant, and of an excellent quality. The discovery of petroleum in the eastern portion of the county has added greatly to its wealth, creating a new industry in its production and export. For many years this county furnished the only oil producing territory in the State. This article of commerce was discovered in this section in 1800, at the time called Seneca or British Oil, and sold in small quantities for medicinal purposes.

As the gentlemen who located the lands for the Ohio Company

foresaw, there has been every advantage developed in facilities for agricultural pursuits, mineral wealth, and all that tend towards a successful competency to the industrious.

MARIETTA.

This, the city of most importance, being the county seat, has realized a steady and satisfactory growth. It is a convenient center for the general distribution of the products and exports of the county, or the exchange of these for the vast supplies necessary for the needs of a large and prosperous community surrounding it. The convenience of the people is greatly faciliated by the numerous lines of railroads intersecting the county, with ample river accommodations, giving more advantages than are generally found in country towns, the industries of the community not being checked during the winter season. The public interest and welfare of the city is in the hands of all its citizens, which results in harmony and a tendency to make the most of the advantages at hand.

Marietta is unusually attractive in the summer months, with its broad streets for pleasant drives; these are well shaded with stately elms and sycamores and maples of large growth. The College Campus is a miniature forest; the City Park, lying along the Muskingum, with smaller parks throughout the city, make it a place of sunshine and shade. The residences are uniformly neat and tasty in appearance, the grounds which surround them large and well-kept, with everything bespeaking comfort, thrift and an intelligent pride. Industry prevails in all vocations, and success and contentment are common blessings.

It is a city of churches and schools, and has sometimes been called "an old college town," which it is in fact. This is an advantage duly appreciated by its citizens, and recognized by strangers who visit here.

as there is an intellectual tone in society always noticeable in college towns, where professors, teachers, scholars are citizens of one and the same community. The college gives a stimulus to all efforts of an educational tendency, so that its advantages are felt on the Academy and the public schools. The latter maintain a standard equal to any in the State. The sturdy New England customs, transplanted here a hundred years ago, are still handed down from sire to son, and are manifest in the even tenor of the life-time of the citizens. They are satisfied with a modest competence, and are not envious of the more stirring cities, which have been built up by the assistance of men nurtured and educated here.

MARIETTA gladly offers the hand of fellowship to her sons and daughters, former sojourners and friends, and through these a welcome is extended to all who may wish to participate in the festivities soon to follow. Accept her hospitality, and view the grand old gateway to the Northwest. Assist in the commemoration of her hundreth anniversary. In this way inaugurate anew an earnest effort to perpetuate the principles secured by the wisdom and sacrifices of our forefathers.

> A century, all hail the time!
>   With quickened pulse we see
> The feasting of our wedding day,
>   The year of jubilee.
> We greetings send to every friend;
>   Dwell with us once again
> Near altar fires, built by our sires,
>   Which steadfast still remain.

The Ohio River.

This was an important factor in the selection of this spot for the new settlement by the Ohio Company, its waters being more accessible than the impenetrable forest, to the band of Pioneers who had the confluence of the two rivers in view as their abiding place. The Indians called it Ohio, meaning in the language of at least two tribes, the fair river, or the fine river. The French explorers said of it, "La belle Riviere,"—meaning beautiful river. It extends along the entire southeastern boundary of the county, a distance of nearly sixty miles. Before the time of railroads it was of vast importance as an avenue to the South and West. It still commands a trade sufficient for a fine line of passenger boats, and numerous craft for a heavy coal and freight traffic.

The stretch of river joining this county is thickly dotted with small, but fertile and beautiful islands, some of these of size sufficient for fine farms and gardens. The names of those adjacent to Washington county are, beginning at Newport,—Grape Island, Middle Island, Three Brothers, Willow Island, Crescent or Kerr's Island, Hutchinson's Island, Neal's Island, Vienna Island, and the historic Blennerhassett Island. These islands greatly enhance the beauties of the lovely scenes, which, in the summer season, are seldom surpassed if they are equaled anywhere else along the course of the river. It is said that the views along this river were to the first settlers a continuous feast of enjoyment. The foliage hung dense, to the margin of the water, often reaching far out over its surface. Sometimes a sunny spot could be found, where a coarse grass, of a lively green color, had taken root and thrived. The deer that came to the sand bars and shallow places were molested only by their own images mirrored in the waters. They slaked their thirst and sped away to the sunny openings for fresh pasturage. The elk and moose shambled down its sloping banks in the silence of the twilight, but soon departed for the deeper density of the woodlands. The wild turkeys called their flocks together among the water grasses, not knowing the danger of the huntsman or his rifle. The buffalo quenched their thirst in their long wanderings and leisurely left its shores after resting from fatigue. Fish played in the sunshine or among the rocks, undisturbed by bait or hook. Even the crows seemed to salute it with a lazy caw when flying above its surface. The Indians paddled their canoes across the placid waters, in search of new hunting grounds beyond the farther shore.

All these made, indeed, a beautiful scene, the beautiful river as it is still called, and it justly merits its name. Not until towards 1800 did the white sail fleck its surface; and it was ten years later before the moving wheel of a steamboat splashed its quiet waters. To the year 1815 there had been less than a dozen moving monuments to the inventive genius of Robert Fulton, coursing their way southward. The first of these was built at Pittsburg in 1811 and passed Marietta in the winter of 1812; the smoke and noise of the boat frightening the children. As late as 1820 not more than a score of steamboats were seeking the traffic of these western waters.

Boat-building was at one time a lively enterprise *at this port.* Instead of river craft, they built sea-going vessels, brigs and schooners. The first of these was the brig St. Clair, built in 1800, commanded by Commodore Whipple, then in the sixty-seventh year of his age. There is a recorded list of twenty-four vessels built here, but the "Embargo Act," of Jefferson, suddenly stopped this industry.

The Ohio river is classed as one of the most important of the United States, its navigable waters and tributaries exceeding five thousand miles. It has two tributaries from this county, with some smaller streams. These are Little Muskingum, above, Muskingum, at Marietta. The Hocking empties just below the county line. Muskingum, in the Indian language, means Elk's Eye, and Hock-Hocking, as it was formerly called, signified "Bottle River."

The area of country drained by the Ohio and its tributaries is estimated to be two hundred thousand square miles, so that incessant and general rains over that portion of the country, or the melting of heavy falls of snow in the mountain regions at the head of its tributaries, result in high floods, some seasons doing great damage. The most notable since the settlement were in 1813, 1832, 1852 and 1884; the latter unprecedented in history and very destructive to property.

The following lines were written by William D. Emerson, (extract of poem.)

TO THE OHIO RIVER.

Eden of rivers, when thy infant rill
   Was yet upon its mother mountain, say,
Who fixed for aye, its hesitating way,—
   Why, on the East didst thou not dance thy way,
And o'er the precipices waste thy spray?
   He who created man, commissioned thee,
And sent thee forth to work thy bed of clay;
   Then bear thy load of waters pure and free,
Until their wealth is stored in the unbounded sea.

A century ago, and what wast thou?
   The red man chased the wild ox o'er the wild,
The birch canoe was then thine only plow,
   And Navigation was an unformed child;
The Indian war-whoop woke thy slumbers, mild,

Thou wert a giant beauty, in the robe
Of untamed nature; cities had not smiled
On blooming farms, and Sol could scarcely probe
The forest, while he bathed in thee, his golden globe.

I love thee, radiant stream; thy banks are free,
The Pioneer has tinged thee with his soul;
His bold and steady mind doth image thee,
Those waters which have borne him to the goal,
Of his far-reaching enterprise, shall roll
Forever past his grave; to history dear:
Thy bells of commerce o'er his sod shall toll,
But not the notes of woe, his spirit's here
And walks the verdant fields, when Spring renews the year.

MILLS.

The old adage, "Happy is the miller that grinds in the mill," could easily have originated with the early settlers. With all their primitive ways and inconveniences, they lacked in nothing more than in the imperfection of their mills, so the miller who had a mill that would grind even slowly was certainly happy, if happiness consists in earthly possessions. Corn was, at first, ground on hand mills, a slow and tedious process, the most popular of these being one of large dimensions called the Army mill. This, being more rapid in execution, was continually "borrowed" by the neighbors. After the hand mills came an era of floating mills, not lasting, as it was found that the current of the rivers was too slow to move a mill-wheel in a very satisfactory manner. A mill run by horse-power was in operation for a long time; this was succeeded by mills built at the rapids of the smaller streams.

The first successful mills by water power were built on Wolf Creek in 1789. These were located about two miles from the mouth of the creek, near Waterford, close enough to Fort Freye for aid, if a retreat was found necessary. These mills were built under the direction of Haffield White, and furnished the grinding for a time for all the settlements, including Marietta, Newport and Belpre, with others; the mills on "Hock-Hocking" afterwards supplying the latter settlement.

Robinson's Mill, 1875.

The site of the first mill on Duck Creek was in close proximity to a farm then owned by Commodore Whipple. The mill there erected was a saw and grist mill. Much of the lumber used in the erection of buildings in Marietta was sawed at this mill, also the lumber in the construction of the boats built at Marietta for Blennerhassett. Adjacent to it were poplar trees in great numbers and of immense size; the lumber of these trees brought but fifty cents per hundred, so that many trees were left to decay upon the ground where they fell.

The last mill in operation on the site of the first mill, was for a long time known as Robinson's Mill. The illustration represents it as it appeared in the year 1875.

The floods of recent years have entirely destroyed this land-mark, as neither the mill or mill-dam is left. From the small beginnings of hand-mills used by the Pioneers grand results have been obtained. Mills now dot the margins of the many streams and splendid structures stand on either bank of the Muskingum near its mouth. Once, where these now stand, the giant Sycamores sent their branches half way across the stream, and the willows fringed the shores until the river presented the appearance of a small creek.

THE BLENNERHASSETTS.

The story of these people is so closely allied with early Marietta history that to omit them, would be to disregard an important episode. The tale tinges so much of romance, that it is next to impossible to believe in the reality of it. Only an outline is here given of what made many pages in history at the time of its existing activity.

About the time of the Declaration of Independence by the United States all nationalities were looking with interest upon the outcome of that event. Some looked with an envious desire and longed for a similar expression in their own governments; none felt the bitter pangs of delay, for themselves, more than the oppressed tenants of Ireland. This same spirit manifested itself in one abundantly able to seek and enjoy the new dispensation here granted. This man was Harman Blennerhassett. He was fitted for the Law, and possessed an inheritance to a fine estate. After his father's death, and his own marriage to Miss Agnew, he soon decided to dispose of his property, which he did, and in the Autumn of 1797, sailed with his wife and intimate friend and school-mate, Emmett, for the United States. He tarried but a fortnight in New York city,—bade his friend farewell and undertook the perilous journey through the wilderness, over mountains, where but ten years before the Ohio settlers had opened the way to the new country, by which the waters of the river they were seeking, gently floated. They came by keel-boat to Marietta, and spent their first winter here. They greatly enjoyed the social atmosphere of New England culture, and too, *their* society was sought and duly appreciated, by people who understood the advantages they had gained by the accession of a family of so refined and courteous manner, who aimed in every way to honor their ancestry which were readily traced to the most illustrious families of the province, from which they had so recently emigrated.

In the early spring-time of 1798, Blennerhassett concluded to purchase a part of an island in the Ohio river and build a residence there rather than reside in Marietta. The purchase was for the upper half of what was then called Backus' Island. He and his wife went immediately to the island, occupying for a time, a deserted block-house, until their own home was completed. This island is twelve miles below Marietta on the line of the Baltimore and Ohio Railroad where it crosses the Ohio river at Parkersburg. It has been called Blennerhassett's island since his occupancy of it and is becoming more and more famous as a resort for pleasure and excursions, in connection with its historic interest. There is nothing remaining, however, of the days of Blennerhassett except some stately sycamores, and the deep well, the walls of which are moss-grown, with luxuriant ferns growing from the crevices.

It must have seemed an enchanted isle, when one reads of the golden, drooping branches of the willow bordering the shores, of the lavish growth of the Eglantine or Wild Brier rose, of the long tendrils of the Honeysuckle, festooning the tall branches of the grand trees of the forest, the 'openings' for the sunlight to gild the cushioned walks covered with moss and wild flowers, the deep, dark corners, cool and damp where luxuriant ferns peacefully grew,—the description alone is exceedingly entertaining. What must it have been after the lavish expenditure of fifty thousand dollars on residence, walks, avenues and all that pertain to the establishing of such a home of luxury. There was nothing need break the quiet solace of these wanderers from their own land but the ripple of the waters over the pebbly shores, the dip of the oar, the quick stroke of the paddle of the canoe, or the songs of the wild birds in their undisturbed carols of delight.

Blennerhassett Mansion.

Nature had been lavish indeed in her adornment and man paused to consider, what he could add, to the already attractive place. It was left for him to dispossess the scene of some of its charms, at a fair recompense, and for eight years this home was mutually enjoyed by the Blennerhassetts, and their many friends. This noble, self-poised manhood finally met its destroyer. The finer balanced tactics of womanhood were sealed by fate when his wife, showed her first courtesy to Aaron Burr and a lady friend, who artfully visited the grounds surrounding their home. She did what any one would probably do, under like circumstances, sent a message by a servant extending to them, in her husband's absence, the hospitality of their mansion. Instead of immediately returning to their boat, they, after assumed deliberation, accepted her invitation, and spent an entertaining evening with her household. The absence of Blennerhassett only delayed Burr's plans for a short time. From Mrs. Blennerhassett, he obtained the address of her husband, when his schemes were partially divulged by a brief correspondence, after which Burr again visited their island home; this time, accompanied by his daughter, the wife of Governor Alston of South Carolina. Her husband soon joined her here, when a mutual confidence and trust pervaded the whole party. It was but a short time until active preparations were engaged in for a temporary abandonment of their lovely home,—as history seems to portray,—merely to join a colony, help organize it, and see it established in the Louisiana country on the " Washita."

Burr left the island, with Alston and his wife in September, 1806, for Lexington, Kentucky. Rumors were soon afloat of a conspiracy against the United States, and the leader of this none other than the late Vice-President when Thomas Jefferson was President. He, it was rumored, was in a deep plot, conspiring against his own government, assisting the breaking in Spanish treaty with the United

States, possibly an interference between these States and Mexico. Many surmises were put put forth but nothing definite was known.

Burr was twice arrested, the first time soon released. On the second, after a long imprisonment and tedious trial, nothing was proven against him. This fact, however, does not greatly detract the mind of the reader from the possibilities of what might have followed had his scheme been allowed to mature, or been left unmolested by state and national interference.

After the first arrest and dismissal of Burr, he returned to Marietta on a hasty errand. He contracted for a number of boats that were to convey Blennerhassett, his family and servants, together with many who had enlisted in a cause, of which they were possibly ignorant of the outcome. These were to go down the Ohio and join others on the way. He left the boats, and the payment of the building of them, to the superintendence of Blennerhassett, and suddenly departed. Rumors were still afloat that a great conspiracy was being concocted. Government detectives were sent out, one visiting here and pleading with Blennerhassett to desist, and turn from the project, but he could not be induced to give it up. He saw that he was closely watched, and anticipated trouble. He left his home on a bleak December night, with boats and men who had come to his assistance. The boats at Marietta were in readiness, and Mrs. Blennerhassett expected to secure these and follow with her children, household effects and servants, immediately.

The strength of the law and the power of the Government was greater than hers or her persuasive words. She returned to find a wild revelry enacting within the walls of luxury,—her own home. Soldiers had been ordered there, who arrived in her absence, and little or no civility was shown the helpless household. She was allowed to leave unmolested, and, with much difficulty as to transportation, secured passage on a boat with a number of young gentlemen from Pittsburg, out for a trip of pleasure and recreation, only taking with her, her children and a few articles hurriedly selected. After many days of great anxiety she succeeded in joining her husband near Natchez. An order from Jefferson to General Wilkinson for the United States, and from Governor Tiffin of Ohio were issued to the State militia simultaneously, in January, 1807, calling troops into active service and ordering militia to be ready to report for duty to thwart every movement of the expedition. These actions so frustrated their plans, whatever they were, that just preceding Burr's second arrest they were altogether abandoned, Burr escaping under disguise.

It was never proven whether the movement was really a conspiracy against the United States, a violation of former treaties with the Government and Spain, an invasion of Mexico, or whether the expedition was to be a peaceful establishing of a colony in the Louisiana country. Burr abandoned the boats and undertook to escape the vigilance of the officers, but was captured in what is now Washington county, Alabama, for a possible treason that was planned and inaugurated in part, in Washington county, Ohio; but under a disguse to those who became victims to the plot, and others who had enlisted in his service.

His trial was in Richmond, Virginia; after a tedious imprisonment and maneuvering there was no further cause for holding him as a prisoner and he was released. He went directly to Europe, where he led an indifferent life, a semi-exile, for twenty-five years, only cherishing the hope, after his return to the United States, of meeting his daughter, Mrs. Alston, who it is supposed was shipwrecked after leaving Charleston, S. C., for New York, as she was never heard of again by husband, father, or friends.

Harman Blennerhassett was arrested and had his trial; nothing was proven against him, and he returned to the then desolate country of the lower Mississippi. His home and property on the island had been confiscated by creditors, and the State of Virginia, and with floods and fire but little was left to attract them again to it. They lived a few years near Natchez, but the war of 1812 blasted all hopes for their future and they again journeyed with their children to a strange land,—this time to Montreal, Canada. From there they went to England, Blennerhassett preceding his wife. Here they finally found refuge with a sister, he waiting for some position by which he might support his family. From there they went to the Isle of Guernsey, where Blennerhassett died in 1831, at the age of nearly sixty-five years.

Mrs. Blennerhassett returned to the United States, and after all their means had been exhausted, was tenderly cared for by former friends. Her children, three boys, not prosperous nor self-sustaining, proved a great addition to her multiplicity of sorrows, and to relate all the care they were to herself and friends would not in any way alleviate her grief for them, and death has claimed them all.

She presented a memorial to Congress asking to be reinstated in a portion of her loss financially. Henry Clay, who had been the attorney for her husband thirty-six years before, then a United States Senator, was conversant with the facts of her misfortune, and earnestly advocated the justness of the claim, and eloquently plead for immediate relief. The relief to her came, but not by man's sensibilities; rather, by the wisdom of the Divine ruler. She died in 1842, and was interred in New York city, under the direction of kind friends, the Emmetts, descendents of the one friend of the Blennerhassetts, and their companion on their sea voyage to America.

Blennerhassett Island still remains historic ground, and there exists through all the years even to-day a reserved sympathy for those, whose tenacity of opinion and confidence in others, led them amiss.

The following poem was written by Mrs. Blennerhassett while in Montreal:

THE DESERTED ISLE.

Like mournful echo from the silent tomb,
    That pines away upon the midnight air,
Whilst the pale moon broke out with fitful gloom,
    Fond memory turns with sad, but welcome care,
    To scenes of desolation and despair;
One bright with all that beauty could bestow,
That peace could shed, or youthful fancy know.

To thee, fair isle, reverts the pleasing dream,
    Again thou risest in thy green attire;
Fresh, as at first, thy blooming graces seem;
    Thy groves, thy fields, their wonted sweets respire;
    Again thou 'rt all my heart could e'er desire.
O why, dear isle, art thou not still my own?
Thy charms could then for all my griefs atone.

The stranger that descends Ohio's stream,
    Charm'd with the beauteous prospects that arise,
Marks the soft isles, that 'neath the glistening beam,
    Dance in the wave, and mingle with the skies;
    Sees also *one*, that now in ruin lies,
Which erst, like fairy queen, towered o'er the rest;
In every native charm by culture dress'd.

There rose the seat where once, in pride of life,
    My eye could mark the queen of rivers flow;

In summer's calmness, or in winter's strife,
  Swol'n with the rains, or baffling with the snow;
  Never again my heart such joy shall know.
Havoc, and ruin, and rampant war, have passed
Over that isle with their destroying blast.

The blackening fire has swept throughout her halls,
  The winds fly whistling throgh them, and the wave
No more in spring-floods o'er the sand-bank crawls;
  But furious drowns in one o'erwhelming grave,
  The hallowed haunts it watered as a slave.
Drive on, destructive flood! and ne'er again
On that devoted isle let man remain.

For many blissful moments there I've known;
  Too many hopes have there met their decay,
Too many feelings now forever gone,
  To wish that thou wouldst e'er again display
  The joyful coloring of thy prime array.
Buried with thee, let them remain a blot;
With thee, their sweets, their bitterness forgot.

And O, that I could wholly wipe away
  The memory of the ills that work'd thy fall;
The memory of that all eventful day,
  When I return'd and found my own fair hall
  Held by the infuriate populace in thrall;
My own fireside blockaded by a band,
That once found food and shelter at my hand.

My children, (O, a mother's pangs forbear,
   Nor strike again that arrow through my soul,)
Clasping the ruffians in suppliant prayer,
   To free their mother from unjust control;
While with false crimes, and imprecations foul,
The wretches, vilest refuse of the earth,
Mock jurisdiction held, around my hearth.

Sweet isle! methinks I see thy bosom torn,
   Again behold the ruthless rabble throng,
That wrought destruction, taste must ever mourn.
   Alas, I see thee now, shall see thee long,
Yet ne'er shall bitter feelings urge the wrong;
That to a mob would give the censure due,
To those that arm'd the plunder-greedy crew.

Thy shores are warm'd by bounteous suns in vain,
   Columbia, if spite and envy spring
To blast the beauty of mild nature's reign,
   The European stranger, who would fling
O'er tangled woods refinement's polishing,
May find (expended every plan of taste,)
His work by ruffians rendered doubly waste.

Isaac and Rebecca Williams.

One hundred years ago, March 26th, 1787, Isaac Williams and his wife moved into a little log cabin, near where Williamstown now stands, opposite this city, in Virginia. The town being named for him. Isaac Williams was a trapper and hunter, and he would hunt and make entries of land, by seeking out a desirable spot, girdle a few trees, plant a patch of corn, and the small amount of time and labor consumed, entitled the person so doing it to *four hundred acres of land.*

These entries were called "Tomahawk Improvements." It is said that an enterprising man could secure a number of these titles in one season, and would sell their "rights and titles," to persons who came into the country afterwards.

These were sold for a few dollars, in cash, but generally the equivalent in traffic of some sort; a rifle was thought a fair price for a four hundred acre tract, at any time, as lands were not then valued for anything except hunting grounds. The greatest advantage in securing these titles was that it gave the holder of them the right of entering one thousand acres of land ajoining these claims, by the payment of a small sum per acre to the State of Virginia, these titles being designated *preemption rights.*

Lands were entered along the Ohio in this State—at that time Virginia claimed a tract in Ohio which was afterwards ceded back to the United States. Mr. Williams married Mrs. Rebecca Martin, daughter of Joseph Tomlinson, of Maryland. She was at the time living with her two brothers, as their house keeper, they, also being fond of hunting, and when off on these expeditions, she would be left entirely alone, but was fearless, and had the courage of man. She would sometimes visit a sister who lived fifty miles farther up the Ohio. On her return from one visit she grew fatigued with paddling her canoe and went ashore and rested until the moon came up, as it was too dark to see distinctly. On her return to the canoe, and in the act of leaping into it, her naked foot rested on the cold dead body of an Indian. She did not lose any time in fainting spells or anything of the sort, saying on her return home "she was very thankful he was not alive."

Her brothers, in consideration of service rendered them, entered four hundred acres of land in Virginia "directly opposite the mouth of the Muskingum," girdling trees on four acres, fencing this and planting it to corn, and building a cabin. This was in the summer of 1773. They spent the summer there, staying so long that their provisions ran low, and they subsisted for two or three months on the boiled meat of turkeys without bread or salt. It was sometime before they could again relish salt in their food. That winter, after a hunt on the Kanawha, they were long detained in their journey home by a great flood in the Ohio, 1774, said to have been equal to that of 1832. The Indians so frequently molested them on Grave Creek that Mr. Williams determined to leave that region, and as there had been a fort, Fort Harmar, erected opposite the land belonging to his wife, he thought this a safe place and came to search it out. He found the clearings that her brothers had made thickly grown over with saplings, which were easier to remove than the large forest trees. He again cleared a spot for a cabin, built it during the winter, and the spring following occupied it with his wife. By the dates it is seen that Mr. and Mrs. Williams, and possibly a few others, have the advantage of one year previous to the settlers of the Ohio Company's purchase. The people of Virginia settling their lands under very different auspices from the early settlers of Ohio.

These early pioneers of Virginia, soon endeared themselves to the Ohio settlers, by their unfailing interest in their welfare, and noble acts of charity which were continually bestowed.

The season of 1789 was short. The early frosts injured the unripened corn, much of it being made unfit for use. In the spring and summer of 1790, the settlers at Marietta suffered for food, especially bread-stuff. This was the year designated by the pioneers as the "Famine," many families having to grind their moldy corn in handmills, and often going many days without even this. Many were glad to get this poor stuff, grind it as aforesaid, make it into mush or porridge, made of sap instead of water.

The story has often been told of Mr. William's benevolent way of distributing his corn, of which he had a large and excellent crop of ripe, sound grain. It does not lose in interest. The unripe corn readily sold as high as two dollars per bushel, and was so scarce that instances are spoken of where children would watch for grains that fell to the floor from the hand-mills, and eat them as if they were delicate and sweet. Mr. Williams proportioned his corn out according to the number in the family, and only took fifty cents a bushel for it, the same price that corn sold at in good seasons when it was plenty.

He was fond of hunting in his old age and often enjoyed the sport of his early manhood.

During the Indian War, from 1791 to 1795, he remained unmolested, building a stockade about his home, for the protection of himself and others. He died in 1820, at the age of eighty-four years, and was buried under the oaks on his own farm. The descendants of the pioneers still cherish the memory, handed down to them of this venerable couple.

Two of Ohio's Governors.

JOHN BROUGH.

"Cleona Farm," as it was formerly called, has its fertile fields lying along the Ohio river on one side and a pleasant country road along its inland frontage on the other. The distance from Marietta is less than one mile. The old homestead on the farm still stands, shaded by maples, and the avenue leading from the farm gate at the road to this, is thickly shaded in summer by maples standing closely together on either side.

On this farm one of Ohio's War Governors, John Brough, was born, in 1811. His father was an Englishman by birth and his mother, who lies in Mound cemetery, was a native of Pennsylvania. After receiving a good English education he added to this latin and the law. He afterwards drifted into the editing and publishing of a newspaper, first at Parkersburg, Va., then Marietta and finally at Lancaster, Ohio. He was Auditor of State, beginning in 1839. Was afterwards in the private capacity of his own affairs, being most of the time in office, in connection with Railroads. He was elected Governor of Ohio in 1863, filling the office for the term beginning 1864, but he did not live to complete the full term of office. He died in Cleveland, Ohio, August 29th, 1866.

RETURN JONATHAN MEIGS, JR.

This gentleman was born at Middletown, Connecticut. Soon after his marriage in 1788, he came to Marietta, where he always resided, except when called away by professional duties, or in response to an election to office. He was the first postmaster at Marietta, thus making him the first in the territory. He served two terms as Governor of Ohio, from the beginning of the term 1810, to the close of the year

1814, thereby covering the period of the war of 1812. He retired to Marietta after the fulfillment of his official duties and died here in 1825. The epitaph on his tombstone records the prominent events of his life, as well as his virtues:

Here lies the body of
RETURN JONATHAN MEIGS,
Who was born at Middletown, Connecticut, 1765,
And died at Marietta, March 29, 1825.
For many years his time and talents were devoted
To the service of his country.
He successively filled the distinguished places of
Judge of the Territory Northwest of the Ohio,
Judge of the Supreme Court of the State of Ohio,
Senator in Congress of the United States,
Governor of the State of Ohio, and
Postmaster General of the United States.
To the honored and revered memory of
An ardent Patriot,
A practical Statesman,
An enlightened Scholar,
A dutiful Son,
An indulgent Father,
An affectionate Husband,
This monument is erected by his mourning widow, Sophia Meigs.

PIONEER ASSOCIATION OF WASHINGTON COUNTY.

This association, with short intervals of suspension has existed since the anniversary of the settlement of the territory. In February, 1789, men belonging to the Ohio Company of Associates, called a meeting, the purport of which was to arrange for a celebration the seventh of April of that year to commemorate the event of the first authorized settlement of the Territory the previous year. The order of exercises were arranged and the following resolution adopted:

Resolved, " That the Seventh of April be forever considered a day of public festival in the Territory of the Ohio Company, as their settlement in this country commenced on that day; and that the directors request some gentleman to prepare an oration to be delivered on the next anniversary."

The following is the

ORATION, DELIVERED AT MARIETTA, APRIL 7, 1789.

BY SOLOMON DROWN, M. D.

"The expectation of so polite and respectable an audience, excited by the novelty of the occasion on which we are assembled, that of celebrating the first anniversary of the settlement of a new and widely extended territory, cannot fail to be productive of diffident emotions in him who has the honor to address you. Feeling his inability to perform, in the manner he could wish, the task allotted him in this day's solemnization, he will, however, strive to re-assure himself from the consideration of the candor he has already experienced, and this last mark of your favorable opinion; an honor to be cherished in his memory with the most affectionate gratitude.

Permit me then most cordially to congratulate you on the auspicious anniversary of the 7th of April, 1788, a day to be remembered with annual festivity and joy; for then this virgin soil received you first;

alluring from your native homes, by charms substantial and inestimable.
 A wilderness of sweets; for Nature here
Wantoned as in her prime, and played at will,
Her virgin fancies, pouring forth more sweet.
Wild above a rule or art,—the gentle gales
Fanning their odoriferous wings, dispense
Native perfumes, and whisper whence they store
Those balmy spoils.

Hail glorious birth-day of this western region! On such a day, in the same beauteous season, ancient poets feigned the earth was first created.

 "In this soft season let me dare to sing
The world was hatch'd by Heaven's Imperial King
In presence of all the year and holidays of spring;
Then did the new creation first appear;
Nor other was the tenor of the year;
When laughing Heaven did the great birth attend,
And eastern winds their wintry breath suspend.
Then sheep first saw the sun in open fields;
And savage beasts were sent to stock the wilds;
Nor could the tender new creation bear
The excessive heats or coldness of the year;
But chilled by winter or by summer fired
The middle temper of the spring regained
When warmth and moister did at once abound,
And Heaven's indulgence brooded on the ground."

First, let us pay our grateful tribute of applause to that firm band, who, quitting their families and peaceful habitations, foregoing all the endearments of domestic life, in the midst of a severe winter, set out on the arduous enterprise of settling this far distant region. And here my inclination would lead me to point their unexampled perseverance in that inclement season; their numerous toils and dangers in effecting the great business of unbarring a selected wilderness, and rendering it the fit abode of man; did not the presence of their worthy leader* prevent me from indulging it.

But of these worthies who have most exerted themselves in promoting this settlement, one, alas! is no more; one whose eloquence, like the music of Orpheus, attractive of the listening crowd, seemed designed to reconcile mankind to the closest bonds of society. Ah! what avail his manly virtues now! Slow through yon winding path his corse was borne, and on the steepy hill interred with funeral honors meet. What bosom refuses the tribute of a sigh, on the recollection of that melancholy scene, when, unusual spectacle, the fathers of the land, the chiefs of the aboriginal nations, in solemn train attended; while the mournful dirge was rendered doubly mournful mid the gloomy nodding grove. On that day even nature seemed to mourn. O Varnum! Varnum! thy name shall not be forgotten, while gratitude and generosity continue to be the characteristics of those inhabiting the country, once thy care. Thy fair fame is deeply rooted in our fostering memories, and,

——Non imber edax, non Agnito impotens,
Posit divmese, aut innumerabilis,
Annorum series, et fuga temporum."†—Hor.

The origin of most countries is lost in the clouds of fiction and romance; and as far up as you can trace their history, you will find they were generally founded in rapacity, usurpation, and blood. It was not

---

*General R. Putnam.
†The force of boisterous winds and moldering rain,
Year after year, an everlasting train,
Shall ne'er destroy the glory of his name.

but by means of wars, horrid wars! that the Israelites gained possession of their long sought promised Canaan; driving before them the nations who had occupied that charming country. Rome itself, imperial Rome, the mistress of the world, was founded by a lawless and wandering banditti, with Romulus at their head, who was continually embroiled with one or other of his neighbors, and war the only employment by which he and his companions expected either to aggrandize themselves, or even to subsist. Singular, then, and before unheard of, are the circumstances of your first establishment, in this extensive territory; without opposition, and without bloodshed. How striking the contrast between such a manner of conducting an important enterprize, and the barbarism of the so much extolled heroic ages! The kind and friendly treatment of the Indians by the first settlers, has conduced greatly to the favorable issue of the late treaty. Such humane conduct, so easy to practice, cannot fail to have great influence, even on savage minds. Nor less the unwearied attention and patient equanimity of his excellency, Governor St. Clair, amid the attacks of a painful disorder, and the delays naturally arising from the discordant interests of unconnected tribes. And here let us commemorate the virtues of the unassuming and most benevolent Mr. John Heckewelder, Moravian missionary among the Delawares. Such is his ascendancy over the minds of the christianized Indians, that to his kind offices in striving to effectuate the above happy event, no small share of praise is to be ascribed. But to whom is this settlement more indebted than to the generous chieftain and other worthy officers of yonder fortress, distinguished by the name of Harmer. With what cheerfulness and cordiality have ye ever entered into every measure promotive of the company's interest. Important is the station ye fill in every respect, and not least in this, that you seem reserved to exhibit mankind a specimen of that military splendor, which ornamented the arms of

America, and would do honor to the troops of any potentate on earth.

The gentle influence of female suavity are ever readily acknowledged by all who make the least pretenses to civilization. Happy in this respect, if we see the least spark of ferocity kindling in our breast, from the wildness of our virtues, to quench the savage principle, and restore us to humanity. Enough cannot be said in commendation of your fortitude and generous resolution, my fair auditors, who apparently made so great a sacrifice in quitting your native homes and endeared connections, to settle in this remote wilderness, while those connections loth to part, were fondly urging every dissuasion from the enterprise, and conjuring up a thousand difficulties that would obstruct your progress, or meet you here. But your laudable perseverance and equanimity have surmounted them all, and instead of being surrounded with howlings of wild beasts, and horrid yells of savages, which ye were warned to expect, on the delightful banks of the Muskingum, ye are favored with the blandishments of polished social intercourse. Are we indeed in a wilderness? The contemplation of the scene before me would almost lead me to distrust my senses. No wonder the gentle Spenser feigned such mingled beauty and elegance, by virtue brightened, could "make a sunshine in the shady grove."

It would take up too much time to detail minutely your progressions in thus far affecting an important settlement. The marks of industry observable on every hand since your arrival, particularly the buildings on Campus Martius (forming an elegant fortress), do you great honor, and lead the admiring stranger to entertain a very flattering opinion of your growing greatness.

> All is the gift of industry: whate'er
> Exalts, embellishes, and renders life
> Delightful. Pensive winter cheered by him,
> Sits at the social fire, and haply hears

> The excluded tempest idly rave along;
> His harden'd fingers deck the gaudy spring,
> Without him summer were an arid waste;
> Nor to the autumnal months could e'er transmit
> The full, mature, immeasurable stores.

Thus fair is the first page of our history, and may no foul blot hereafter stain the important volume which time is unfolding in this western world. But may it prove worthy, fraught with worthy deeds, to be rescued from the final conflagration, by some bright cherub's favoring arm, and displayed to the view of approving spirits in the realms of bliss.

This country will afford noble opportunity for advancing knowledge of every kind. A communication with all nations will enable you to introduce the most useful and excellent scientific improvements, which are to be found in every kingdom and empire on earth. Effectual measures have been taken by congress for cultivating and diffusing literature among the people, in appropriating large tracts of land for the establishment of schools, and a university. The institution of a public library would be of great benefit to the community, not only by affording rational amusement, and meliorating the disposition, but by giving those who have not a liberal education an opportunity of gaining that knowledge which will qualify them for usefulness. * *

But that for which this country will ever be most estimable, is, that under the auspices of firmly established liberty, civil and religious, and the mild government of national laws, every circumstance invites to the practice of husbandry, that best occupation of mankind, which is the support of human life, and the source of all its true riches. Delightful region! bordering on the majestic Ohio, the most beautiful river on earth, watered also by other large and navigable streams; favored with an excellent climate and fertile soil, which well cultivated, is a rich treasure to every family that is wise enough to be contented with living nobly independent. It is in such charming retreats, at a distance from the tumultuous hurry of the world, that one relishes a thousand innocent delights, and which are repeated with a satisfaction ever new. In those extensive and delightsome bottoms, where are seen so many different species of animals and vegetables, there it is we have occasion to admire the beneficience of the Great Creator. There it is, that at the gentle purling of a pure and living water, and enchanted with the concert of birds, which fill the neighboring thickets, we may agreeably contemplate the wonders of nature, and examine them all at our leisure. It is amid such happy, rural scenes, fanned by gentle breezes, wafting fragrance o'er the blossomed vale. that health and rejuvenescency of soul are indulged to mortals—the choicest of the favors of heaven."

* * * * * * * * * * *

The day was held in almost sacred reverence, and duly kept for many years succeeding the settlement, at least until the rapid increase of population lessened the interest in the event, because a majority of the citizens were of those who came, after the trials by war, famine, and pestilence had ceased. There was always a public feast and address, after these all maaner of innocent sports were indulged in, such as base-ball, foot-ball, shooting at a mark, foot-racing, wrestling and dancing. The young people often exchanged visits between Belpre and Marietta, and making the journey by boats. These and similar amusements, are yet in vogue at some of the Pioneer celebrations of to-day,— thereby aiming to carry out the idea of amusements in days of Lang Syne. The day was always considered a holiday for the giving and returning social visits, and in 1838, a general and enthusiastic meeting was held, to celebrate the fiftieth anniversary of the settlement.

In 1841, there was organized the Marietta Historical Association with Ephraim Cutler, President, William R. Putnam, ⎫ Arius Nye, Vice President, John Mills, ⎬ Curators. Caleb Emerson, Cor. Secretary. A. T. Nye, ⎭ Arius Spencer Nye, Rec. Sec'y.

The object of this association was "to establish a library, cabinet, and repository worthy the oldest settlement in Ohio." This organization continued many years, the members devoting much time in collecting historical facts and incidents, some of which give us the only history we have of the early days of the settlers. The college finally became the receptacle of such as was in this way collected, this being under constant care and a place for safe keeping.

In 1866, Frances Dana Gage wrote a poem, dedicated "to the living members of the Pioneer Association of Washington county." Her birth-place is but a short distance up the Muskingum river. As a tribute to her, as well as other Pioneers, extracts of the poem are here given:

    Oh, a monument the grandest
      Is Ohio now I ween,
    Of the power of human progress
      That the world hath ever seen;
    For the children's feet that pattered
      O'er the cabin's puncheon floor
    Now walk her marble State House,
      We, two million souls or more.

    Who hath felled the mighty forests?
      Who hath reaped the golden grain?
    Who hath sent the thundering rail-car
      Through the mountain, o'er the plain?

Who hath built the people's school-house,
 Filled with music every dale,
Where once the Indian's war-whoop
 Heard its echo in the vale.

All honor to the heroes
 Who, with hearts so strong and true,
Conquered forest, beast, and Indian
 In these Western wilds, when new.
Not with wicked, vain ambition
 Not with war-shrieks, fierce and wild
But with reaping-hook and plow-share
 Making home for wife and child.

With ax, and plow, and hammer,
 With reaper and the mill,
The school-house and the church-spire
 Tell of Progress, onward still.
Opening wide to every nation
 Every door to wealth and fame;
Making tyrants fear and tremble,—
 The oppressed ones bless their name.

The Pioneer Society, as now existing, was organized in 1870, with W. F. Curtis, Recording Secretary, which office he has since held. The officers at this time—1887—are:

        Douglas Putnam, President;
        William Glines, Vice President;
        W. F. Curtis, Recording Secretary;
        R. M. Stimson, Corresponding Secretary;
        F. A. Wheeler, Treasurer.

There has been a meeting on each anniversary covering this period, Mr. A. T. Nye, Col. John Mills, Col. William R. Putnam and Samuel Shipman, manifesting untiring interest until their deaths.— Other members remembered as always present, were William Glines, Henry Fearing, Dr. I. W. Andrews, Col. E. S. McIntosh, Beverly, William P. Cutler, L. J. P. Putnam, and Dr. B. F. Hart. The Pioneer Society of Marietta covers an interesting period of time. The one hundred years of its existence is a grand epoch on the pages of history. Its members, the lives of a few, covering nearly a century, and a number of them counting three-fourths of a century as their years, have seen the Northwest Territory redeemed from a wilderness, by the rapid increase of population, and all that follows with this; not only the Northwest Territory, whose western boundary was the Mississippi river, but on and on the triumphal car of civilization has rapidly penetrated the west to the broad Pacific, connecting the extremes of this continent. From this country, with its vast sea coast, richly laden vessels traverse the mighty waters east and west to every seaport of the globe.

The Pioneer Society of Washington county hope to secure a Memorial worthy the commemoration of the events herein mentioned. This, to perpetuate the memories of the soldiers of the Revolutionary war, who came here also as first settlers, of those who assisted in the enactment of the Ordinance which stands as the event pre-eminent in the history of this nation, of the founders and defenders of the State and frontier, of the first settlers, and as a recognition of the many sacrifices made that the present generations might live in peace and prosperity. May they secure a tribute worthy the cause, and worthy the vast populace it will represent.

The men in activity a hundred years ago have builded their own monument, greater, grander than others can possibly achieve; for the opportunity, such as theirs, passed by with their lives. It is only left for their fellow-men, their descendants, to join hand in hand in the perpetuation of their memory. Let such a Memorial be given unto the watchful care and keeping of those familiar with the lives of these men, who remain as descendants, on the spot made hallowed by their memory.

The Centennial Monument Association has been incorporated under the laws of the State, and is engaged in raising funds for a monument to the Pioneers. During the exercises of the Centennial celebration, an hour will be set apart, on Saturday, April 7th, for the laying of the corner stone of this Monument, by the President of the United States.

The Board of Trustees of the Association consists at present of the following gentlemen:

Douglas Putnam,   Henry Fearing,
I. W. Andrews,   George Dana,
Wm. P. Cutler,   E. R. Alderman,
Beman Gates,   John Mills.

The officers are: Douglas Putnam, President; Beman Gates. Treasurer; R. L. Nye, Secretary.

In order to assist in carrying out an entertaining programme for the Centennial Celebration, the ladies of Marietta have organized a Woman's Auxiliary to the Pioneer Association, and are actively engaged in securing funds to meet the expenses of that event.

The Pioneers—1788.

"God speed," in the homes of New England,
 "God bless you," the earnest reply,—
Then, cheer upon cheer, gladly echoed
 A thrilling farewell and good bye.
The Pioneer band then departed,—

The steady, the strong and the great,—
Westward, the watchward, accepted
　With firmness, a New England trait.
Great in manhood and bitter privations,
　With strength to endure to the last,
They battled with sturdy convictions,
　Wherever their fortunes were cast.
In descending the beautiful river
　On a mission, the motive sublime,
Their boat guided fearlessly onward
　To an epoch, recorded by Time.
Their boat held the pulse of a nation
　A nation to them yet unborn,
They endured, for the sake of their offspring,
　And pity, they treated with scorn.
They came to the river Muskingum,
　Then hidden almost from their view,
They felled the dense forest about them,
　They toiled in the sun and the dew.
By the stroke of the ax and the hammer,
　By toil, to these men,—not a dream—
Their gardens bloomed forth in their grandeur
　By the banks of the beautiful stream.
In the Autumn the harvest was golden,
　Out-sprung from the rich virgin soil,—
The workers were pleased with their effort,
　Well repaid for the summer's hard toil.
Men, with their wives and their children,
　Came here, and enjoyed in their way
Their homes in the cabins and forest

Which are gone now, to dust and decay.
Hard struggles ensued with the savage
　So treacherous, that no one could tell
If the day would bring sadness upon them
　Or, whether in peace they might dwell.
They cleared up these far-reaching valleys,
　These hills, and the more fertile plain,—
Their churches, and schools, to defenders
　It is hoped will forever remain.
Let us meet, and sincerely revere them,
　Their memory keep sacred and true;
While their ashes lie buried around us
　Revive thus their spirits anew.

[1883.]

Marietta College.

This college was founded in the year 1835. The charter provides for the establishment of a seat of learning; a general clause which covers the whole scope for a liberal diffusion of knowledge says: "For the education of youth in the various branches of useful knowledge." There has never been but one slight amendment to its orignal charter, which was in regard to the increase in the number of its trustees, and possibly in the manner of electing officers.

The buildings are located on high ground in the most desirable and central part of the city. The grounds consist of one full city square or block.

As early as 1790 the idea of providing funds for schools was promulgated, and money was then appropriated for these in Marietta, Belpre, and Waterford. In 1797 a plan was submitted by which a regular academy was established, and thus originated the Muskingum Academy, the first seat of learning in the Northwest Territory under any corporation or company. This continued until about the time of the incorporation of the present college, whose charter members were Luther G. Brigham, John Cotton, Caleb Emerson, John Mills, John Crawford, Arius Nye, Douglas Putnam, Jonas Moore, and Anselm T. Nye. Mr. Crawford and Mr. Nye soon resigning. This college is free from state influence or control, and is the out-growth of men schooled in the War for Independence and others nurtured in Harvard, Yale, Dartmouth, Brown, and other eastern colleges. There is ample room for the accommodation of a large number of students, it is thoroughly equipped with every facility for the progress of the student, in way of libraries and apparatus for experiments in the various branches.

The first building or dormitory was erected in 1833, for the "Marietta Collegiate Institute and Western Teacher's Seminary." Two years later a new charter was obtained, allowing the conferring of degrees, and making it more substantial, in regard to amendments and repeals. The middle building was completed in 1850. In this are the halls of the college societies. The Hildreth and Slocomb collections and a superior cabinet of specimens interesting to the geological and natural history student; also the recitation rooms.

The upper or library building was erected in 1870 by the Alumni of the college. This contains the libraries of the college societies and the college library; also the chapel, which is called Alumni Hall.

The Alumni of this college, with few exceptions, have not been men of wealth; consequently through that source it has not increased its endowment fund rapidly, neither have bequests been frequent. Benevolent men have supported it generously, so that with a careful fore-sight of its worthy President and the frugal management of its Trustees, there has been a safe and steady increase of funds that has been very satisfactory to the friends of the college, the alumni and citizens of Marietta who have a just pride in this seat of learning.

The first President was Rev. Joel H. Linsley, D. D., from 1835 to 1846. He was succeeded by Rev. Henry Smith, D. D., LL. D., until 1855, when Rev. Israel Ward Andrews, D. D., LL. D., accepted and held the honored position for thirty years, with great judgment, honor and distinction. In 1885 Hon. John Eaton was chosen, and is now the President; an educator of wide reputation in this country and abroad.

A resident of this city, William D. Emerson, in 1836, penned the following :

> Here, where two meeting rivers fringe the plain
> O'er which the semi-circling green hills tower,
> The Pioneer City stands; its streets a chain,

In grace, enfolds each cottage tree and flower;
Here, learning loves to build her shady bower,
And like a magnet, draws the mind from far;
Giving that mind its own magnetic power,
Freighting the mental and the moral car,
And sprinkling all the West with many a radiant star.

This college, like all others, suffered greatly, in the breaking up of classes, during the War of the Rebellion; the average number not again appearing until 1870. There cannot be a more fitting tribute to the student soldiers than was given, in an address, by the President, I. W. Andrews, entitled "Marietta College in the War." An extract is here given:

"Of those who settled on the lands of the Ohio Company within the first few years, probably sixty had held commissions as officers in the war for independence. It was by the descendants of these men that the college at Marietta was founded, and they have been its most generous supporters. Twelve, at least, of its Trustees have been the lineal descendants of the pioneers. The atmosphere of the place was thus of necessity historical, and the students of the institution, graduates and undergraduates, in responding so heartily to the call for troops in 1861, exhibited that patriotic loyalty which might have been expected from those who had been educated under such influence. The descendants of the pioneers will not be ashamed of the deeds and sacrifices of those of their number who went forth to battle in behalf of their country. The college will never cease to cherish the memory of her youthful sons who attested the sincerity of their patriotism with their blood. And she will ever hold in high honor those whom a kind Providence has spared amid all the perils of war, and permitted to return and enjoy the rich blessings of that Union which their valor helped to secure."

The Marietta Academy.

The building is situated on the college campus, and is under the direct supervision of the Trustees of the college. It is a college preparatory school, and the students can have access to the libraries, laboratory and museum of the college. The Professors are Martin R. Andrews, M. A., Principal, assisted by Allen E. Beach, B. A., as tutor in Latin and Greek.

Marietta Observatory.

In the summer of 1880 several gentlemen of Marietta formed an association for the purpose of securing to this city, an observatory of sufficient accuracy for astronomical researches and correct calculations. The carrying out of their plans in the construction and equipment of the building was given to one of their number, Mr. W. C. Gurley.

The telescope, for general observation is not large, the aperture is six and one-half inches, with a focal length of nine feet. This is unsurpassed in faultless definition, and is exceedingly satisfactory. It was mounted, temporarily, and first used in the observation of the transit of Venus, December 6, 1882. There is every facility offered for astronomical observations, a Diffraction, Spectroscope, a four inch telescope with finder, mounted on a tripod, a solar prism, and all the etcetera for complete calculations in the siderial heavens. The Driving Clock is surperior in workmanship and operation. To all these have been added a Siderial Clock, purchased of Marietta College; a clock of the same make—Kessels—is the standard time keeper in the National Observatory, Washington, D. C. The rooms are furnished as parlors or for study, and are pleasant and comfortable.

NEWSPAPERS.

The first newspaper in the county of Washington, was published November 30, 1801, called the "Ohio Gazette and the Territorial and Virginia Herald." In 1805, the name was changed to the Ohio Gaette and Virginia Herald. It had a succession of names and proprietors for a number of years. In 1839, Beman Gates, still a resident of this city, with others, began the publication of the Intelligencer, which in 1842 absorbed the Gazette and its property. The Gazette was the successor to the first paper published. Thus the Intelligencer came to be heir to the succession. In 1862 the property passed into the hands of R. M. Stimson, also a resident of this city, and the name was changed to The Marietta Register. In 1872, the Register was purchased by E. R. Alderman, who has associated his sons, E. S. and A. D. Alderman. It has been published as a semi-weekly since 1883, and has always advocated the principles of the Republican party. The office has in its possession still a portion of the press on which the paper was printed in 1801.

The Marietta Times was established in 1864, by Walter S. Hood, who was suceceeded in 1871 by S. M. McMillen, the present proprietor. It is successfully managed, and is an exponent of the Democratic party.

The Marietta Zeitung, conducted in the interest of the German population of the county, has been since 1869 under the management of Jacob Mueller, the firm now being Jacob Mueller & Son.

The Marietta Leader was established in 1881, is Republican in politice, and now controlled by T. F. Davis.

The College Olio, edited by students of Marietta College, is the channel for educational topics. It is published semi-monthly during the college term.

Harmar Cemetery.

Not far from the banks of the Muskingum river, a few paces north of the town, and the site of Fort Harmar, is a burial place known as the Harmar cemetery. It is a secluded spot of not more than four acres of ground, lying at the base of a rugged hill that rises abruptly far above it. The marble shafts stand out in bold relief summer and winter, the deep, dark green of fir and spruce and the grassy slope ever forming a contrasting back-ground for the white purity of the marble.

Aside from its natural beauties there is little to attract strangers within the gates, until it is known that this is the oldest cemetery in the State of Ohio, and—thereby in the "Territory Northwest of the Ohio,"—that was formally reserved for such a purpose and is still in use. This plat of ground was so reserved by the Ohio Company in the year 1796. Ground was reserved in Marietta at the same time, but the bodies there laid to rest were long ago reinterred, and the place abandoned as a cemetery.

Many of the pioneers and early settlers, who sleep the sleep of unnumbered years, lie in the Harmar cemetery. Among them Paul Fearing, Joseph Gilman, Joseph Bosworth, and Christopher Burlingame. Recently a handsome granite shaft has been erected to the memory of B. D. Fearing, Brigadier General in the war of the Rebellion. The first interments on the frontier were of soldiers whose deaths occurred while they were stationed at Fort Harmar; where these graves were located or discovered the remains were re-interred in other burial lots, that of Englehard Hopper in Oak Grove.

Mound Cemetery.

The spot of ground so-called was first reserved and intended as a public park, to be designated as Marie Antoinette Square. Communications were sent to the Queen of France, asking the privilege of so commemorating her name and kindly interest in this country and government. Ill health caused a final delay in her reply so it was afterwards called Mound Square.

View of Mound Cemetery.

In 1791, Joseph Gilman, Rev. Daniel Story, and Jonathan Hart were appointed a committee to lease the public squares to individuals designating the care and ornamentation to be bestowed upon them.

The Mound Square was leased to General Rufus Putnam for twelve years, provided "he would surround the whole square with mulberry trees, with an elm at each corner. The base of the mound to be encircled with weeping willows, with evergreens on the mound. The circular parapet outside the ditch to be surrounded with trees, all within the square to remain undisturbed by the plow, and seeded down to grass, the whole enclosed with a post and rail fence." It might also be added here that the greater part of the ancient earth works, of which the mound is a part, were so reserved for a great many years; and two large *elevated* squares of pre-historic origin are still the property of the city and handsome specimens of the race known as the Mound Builders. Trustees were appointed to carry out the design of the Ohio Company until such a time as the town would be incorporated, and take charge of and care for them.

Whether the transactions were ever carried out by General Putnam or not is left for the inference of the reader, as there are no indications now of trees being planted as designated by the lease. Dr. Hildreth elsewhere says that Mound Square was reserved by the Ministerial Trustees of Marietta at an early day and leased to the town, with about four acres of ground, as a public burying ground; the first interment taking place September 30, 1801, that of the body of Colonel Robert Taylor. Captain Josiah Munro, a Revolutionary soldier, died one month earlier and is now buried in Mound Cemetery, but was reinterred from an abandoned lot. The mound is near the centre of the square, is a perfect circle at the base, which is one hundred and fifteen feet in diamiter, with a parapet encircling it, broad enough for a carriage way. This leaves a ditch or moat between the base of the mound and this circle, about sixteen feet broad. Large forest trees grow upon every part of it. Stone steps have been placed upon the North side, so that persons can ascend to the top with ease, and can there secure a fine outlook; scanning a portion of the Ohio river, the extreme points visible being nearly seven miles apart. The perfect proportions, the great size, the peculiar formation, might be all there is to admire. This is not all, to citizens who have beheld it a lifetime. They confess an admiration for its perfect symmetry a sincere pride in its existance, and justly consider it the monument of two distinct races: The time and activity of the builders not clearly known, and of the other, sooner forgotten but for this conspicuous reminder, around whose base in encircled the burial place of the heroes of four wars. It is then the Nation's pride, the pride of the State, of the commonwealth, emanating from the Northwest Territory, as well as a place reserved by the citizens of this county and city. There is not, in all probability, a cemetery, aside from those in close proximity with the battle grounds, where rest so many soldiers, and especially soldiers of the Revolutionary War.

Would that it could be told in whispers, some of these men died too poor to provide their own tomb-stones; no fault of theirs, and no dishonor, but rather a credit that has long stood in their favor, and should ever be recognized. The best years of their lives were spent in defense of their country. Their families impoverished by the cause and continuation of the war. They accepted this western wilderness as a compensation for services rendered their country, were soon involved in war here, with the Indians, and in their last efforts to provide for their families gave up their lives, and lie buried within the limits of Washington county, half of the names here given, in Mound Cemetery. The list is not complete, but given as far as has been ascertained.

Revolutionary Soldiers—Mound Cemetery: Commodore Abraham

Whipple, General Rufus Putnam, General Joseph Buell, General Benjamin Tupper, Major Ezra Putnam, Colonel Ichabod Nye, Colonel Ebenezer Sproat, Colonel William Stacey, Captain Josiah Munro, Captain Nathaniel Salstanstall, Captain William Mills, Lieutenant Joseph Lincoln, Mr. Nathaniel Dodge, Mr. Ephraim Foster.

General James M. Varnum, Colonel Robert Oliver, Captain Joseph Rogers, and a number of others—names unknown—re-interred in Oak Grove cemetery, near by. In Harmar cemetery are Christopher Burlingame, Joseph Bosworth, and others, names not ascertained.

Belpre:—Major Robert Bradford, Major Oliver Rice, Colonel Nathaniel Cushing, Colonel Daniel Fisher, Colonel Silas Bent, Colonel Israel Putnam, Captain Zebulon King, Captain William Dana, Captain Jonathan Stone, Captain Nathan Goodale,* William James, Benjamin Miles, Lieutenant Jonathan Haskell, Sherabiah Fletcher. Waterford:—Major Haffield White, Major Asa Coburn, Major Dean Tyler, Lieutenants Neale McGaffy, William Gray, Benjamin Converse. Newport:—Colonel Ebenezer Battelle, Oliver Woodward. Barlow:—Samuel Chapman. Muskingum Tp.:—Captain Jonathan Devol. Watertown:—Daniel Davis. Captain Benjamin Brown probably at Amesville, formerly in Washington county.

Judge Burnett, in speaking of the Marietta colony of which the above list is a part, says:

"After having spent the most valuable period of their lives in the army, enduring every species of exposure, fatigue and suffering; they were dismissed to their homes, if they were so fortunate as to have any, with nothing but empty promises, which have never been realized; and most of them with broken or impaired constitutions. The certificates they received as evidence of the sums due them from the country were almost valueless. They were bought and sold in the

---

*Captured by Indians.

market at two shilling and six pence for twenty shillings; and as late as 1788, they were only worth five shilling in the pound. They were honorable, high-minded men, whose feelings rebelled at the thought of living in poverty among people of comparative wealth, for the protection of which, their own poverty had been incurred. Under the influence of that noble feeling hundreds of those brave men left their friends, and sought retirement on the frontiers, where no invidious comparisons could be drawn between wealth and poverty; and where they became involved in the hazardous conflicts of another war."

The friends and descendants of a number have paid fitting tributes to their dead, by the erection of tablets to their memory, replacing those gone to decay, and in many ways manifesting an interest in the preservation of their deeds of valor and patriotism.

The soldiers of the war of 1812 are well represented in this cemetery, among them, Governor Return J. Meigs, Jr., (War Governor from 1810 to 1814), Col. John Thornily, Major Alexander Hill, Major William Hart, Major John Clark, Captain Timothy Buell, Jason Curtis, Joseph L. Reckard, Sen., Wyllis Hall, Jasher Taylor, Stephen Daniels, Harry Cogswell, Robert Wells.

The long list of names of the soldiers of the war of the Rebellion, would only revive heart-aches if here published; their names have been preserved, and will stand out as boldly a hundred years hence, as they do to-day. The citizens of this county have erected a fine monument to their soldiers who fell in the late war.

Soon after the close of the war of the Rebellion, in 1865, there was an association of gentlemen organized for the purpose of erecting a monument to the soldiers of Washington county. A charter was granted and immediate action taken, for securing funds for the erection of a monument. One year from that time, something over sixteen hundred dollars were reported as in the treasury. Subscriptions continued to increase until 1873, when over four thousand dollars had been secured. The monument was completed at a cost of five thousand dollars, and stands on the City Park, as a handsome testimonial of the citizens of Washington county to her deceased soldiers for whom it was erected. There were over four thousand soldiers enlisted during the war from this county. Two camps for the enlistment and rendezvous of soldiers at Marietta, Camp Putnam, named for Gen. Rufus Putnam, and Camp Tupper, for Gen. Benjamin Tupper.

Through the patriotism of its soldiers, and the loyalty of its citizens, the principles of the founding of this government, were preserved and a national independence maintained such as does not exist on another portion of this globe.

There were sixty commissioned officers among the early settlers of Marietta. It is shown that in Mound cemetery, in this city of the dead, rest soldiers of the war for Independence, the promoters of the Ordinance of 1787, the men of the Ohio Company who were the advance guard of a vast commonwealth, soldiers of the war of 1812, of the Mexican war, and heroes of the last war, soldiers and civilians all equal in death, lie side by side, at the base of the majestic mound whose sphinx-like silence reveals not the history of the past. Some have fitting monuments to mark their graves, others have none. The government and the people representing it, and enjoying its provisions, know their just obligations. Like these men, now resting from their labors,—the nation was poor which was its excuse for withholding that which it was willing to bestow upon from those deserving its recognition. May it now be considered a privilege to assist in one grand monument to their memory that will be imperishable in the coming years, and serve as a reminder of the valor and patriotism of the heroes of one hundred years ago now sleeping in Ohio soil.

A few selections have been made from tomb-stones, to show the character of the departed.

These men, associates in Massachusetts, also, in the formation and carrying out of the plans of the Ohio Company, now rest in the same cemetery:

Gen' Rufus Putnam,
a Revolutionary officer and
the leader of the colony which
made the first settlement in the
Territory of the Northwest at
Marietta April 7, 1788.
Born April 9, 1738.
Died May 4, 1824.

Gen' Benjamin Tupper,
Born
At Sharon Mass' in 1738
Died
June 7, 1792 aged 54 years.

Samuel P. Robbins.

This stone, nearly destroyed by frosts. The epitaph gone, but it is known that he was pastor of the Congregational church from 1806 to 1823. He planned the present church and gave liberally towards its erection. He established the first Bible society here, and died esteemed by all who knew him.

Here also are the tombstones of Rev. Hiram Gear, as minister of Baptist church, and Rev. Greenberry R. Jones, "a faithful and successful minister of the Methodist church."

In
Memory of
REV' DANIEL STORY, D. D.
Died
at Marietta
Dec' 30, 1804
aged
49, years.
A native of Boston Massachusetts.
Educated at Dartmouth College.
He was the first minister of Christ
who came to Labor in the vast field
known as the Northwest Territory,
excepting the Moravian Missionaries.
Came to Marietta 1789, as a
Religious Teacher under an arrangement
with the Ohio Company. Accepted a call
from the Congregational Church and
was ordained as their pastor, at
Hamilton, Massachusetts
August 15, 1798.

SACRED
to the memory of
COMMODORE ABRAHAM WHIPPLE,
Whose name, skill and courage
will ever remain the pride
and boast of his country.
In the late Revolution he was the
first on the seas to hurl defiance at proud Britain,
gallantly leading the way to wrest from
the mistress of the ocean her scepter
and there to wave the star-spangled banner.
He also conducted to the sea the
first square-rigged vessel ever built on the Ohio,
opening to commerce
resources beyond calculation.

His last years were spent in a very retired and unassuming manner, not even military honors at his burial. Though, as an old settler says, "the grand artillery of heaven gave him a royal salute;" as there was a terrific thunder storm while the procession was going to the grave.

Additional names of Revolutionary Soldiers, Waterford Township.—Benjamin Shaw, Andrew Story, David Wilson, Abel Sherman, Allen Devol.

EPITAPHS CONDENSED.

General Joseph Buell, stationed at Fort Harmar, 1786. One of the permanent settlers in 1787. Interred in Mound cemetery.

Colonel Ebenezer Sproat, the first sheriff of the county, and the first one of the Pioneers to land upon Ohio soil.

Captain Nathaniel Salstanstall, born in New London, Connecticut. Died 1807. Was first commandant, Fort Trumbull during the Revolutionary war.

Nahum Ward came to Marietta, 1809, was for many years an agent for the Ohio Company. He spent a long and respected life in this city.

Anselm Tupper Nye, born in Campus Martius, November 9, 1797. Died October 5, 1881.

Colonel John Mills, born at Marietta, December 2, 1795. Died March 14, 1882. The entire life time of these two men was spent in Marietta as honored and respected citizens.

The names of Brough, Worthington, Case, Tod, Greene, Peirce, True, Dodge, Woodbridge, Putnam, Nye, McIntosh, and Wheeler, are old time familiar names. Those of to-day—they are all there—side by side with the dead of one hundred years ago, they need not be mentioned, but may their memory be recalled as the years roll on towards another century. A cemetery like this, dating back so far, has both local and general interest. Those who visit it, must certainly be impressed, with veneration towards its surroundings and name it hallowed ground. May the dust of ages past lie undisturbed and every passer-by be reminded of his duty in the care and keeping of this honored and revered spot.

There are two other burial places. The Catholic cemetery is at the northern terminus of Third street. This is thickly set with tombstones, and is a place of interment for the members of the Catholic church from different sections of the county.

Oak Grove, the new cemetery of the city, contains about thirty-five acres of ground, is a bright, cheery landscape, and is modern in appearance, having graded drives through the grounds. The whole consisting of hill, valley, and plain, giving persons a variety in the selection of lots. The first person buried in this cemetery was Timothy Cone in April, 1864, in the eighty seventh year of his age.

Ancient Earth Works.

Washington County Woman's Home.

The century will close the pages of local history for this vicinity, with the addition of a noble charity, one wholly supported by private donations. It was evident, after the close of the War of the Rebellion that the plans in many homes were materially changed. Mothers, who had given their all, their sons, who were to be their main support, who crushed with sorrow, in their declining years scarcely knew which way to turn for aid.

The Government did much to relieve dependent ones, and a strong sentiment of charity was inaugurated, such as this country had never before experienced. The sin of intemperance frequently joined issues with other causes, to more completely wreck once happy homes, and turned helpless women upon strangers and friends for aid. Much was given, more required. As the years swept by, the greater the demand upon the public for assistance.

A refuge, or home, in this locality seemed a necessity. A lady, an invalid, often counseled with her friends, in regard to the establishment of such a charity. This not being perfected at her death, her husband, now deceased, took the preliminary steps for carrying out her wishes, by enlisting the attention of a number of benevolent women in the cause. An organization was completed in 1880, and the first effort towards the establishment of the Woman's Home was then inaugurated.

An incorporate act was provided, a board of gentlemen appointed as Trustees, and as many ladies as a Board of Managers. They were urged to begin the canvas at once for subscriptions, and encouraged to believe that material aid would develop in their behalf.

Mrs. Ewing and others took an active interest in the work, both in the cities of Marietta and Harmar and through the county. The cause was so impartially presented that the ladies engaged in the work felt justified in making an outlay in the purchase of grounds. In their effort to secure a building site, two gentlemen, Mr. Douglas Putnam, of Harmar, and Mr. M. P. Wells, of Marietta, came to their assistance, and each donated a full city lot, lying side by side. With these ample gifts came great encouragement, and a building of moderate dimensions was at once constructed. This is sufficient in size to fill the present demands, and is so planned that extensions can be easily added. It is cheerful, comfortable, and well adapted to the purposes for which it is intended.

When the Home was completed, friends came forward with supplies, and showed their confidence in the management by contributing liberally in the furnishing.

The aid most expected, came not, but the prayers of a Christian woman are being answered, in the fulfillment of her earnest desires. The Home was formally opened in November, 1885, with two inmates. A number, who had applied for aid, were relieved of earthly anxieties by death, in the two or three months previous to the completion of the Home.

This institution has only the development that two years can show, but it has been successful in every particular. Four inmates, women over seventy years of age, are enjoying every possible comfort of a home. Others are contemplating the acceptance of the same privileges at such a time as best suits their own convenience. It is a grand retreat from poverty and want for deserving women, who have spent a life of hard work, but through no fault of their own, now need the help of the charitable.

The Home has been founded, established, and sustained by private charity. Its charter is such that it can never become an institution to be supported by taxation. The funds are provided by a " ways and means" plan that might prove uncertain, though it never has failed yet. The whole support is covered by private donations, coming at no stated time, often when least expected, but most needed; singular circumstances occurring in this way. Other means of securing funds are by fairs, festivals, and any of the ordinary ways in common use, but there is nothing permanent, as yet, towards a certain and assured support.

The property has a valuation of upwards of four thousand dollars, has been liberally sustained, but like the first years of nearly all charitable institutions the Home is yet struggling for recognition, and in need of a more permanent basis for support. Five hundred persons who would pledge themselves to pay one dollar each year as annual members, would secure an ample income with which to meet all present needs, and also be adding a small per cent to a reserve fund, to be used when needed. With a population in the county of over forty thousand it is expected soon to reach this number.

"*There were women in those days.*" * * * * * * * *
History records the names of but few of the pioneer women, once in our midst. In that time they were known, as the daughters of their fathers, the wives of their husbands, the sisters of their more eminent brothers. How could they be more fittingly memorialized than in having this charity, this gift to aged and respected women, which is managed entirely by women, dedicated as a testimonial to their courage and patriotism, for they possessed both.

Let this appeal go forth to the women of Washington county. Cannot there be secured memorial bequests, either in remembrance of women who came here as wives of the early settlers, or in recognition of the sentiment now more clearly shown, for the general advancement of women. In the name of these women and this grand truth let this one, the only charitable institution of the county, receive new impulse and with it, rich blessings. Let a new exertion be put forth, in filial regard and love, remembrance and veneration, for the pioneer women of the infant State of Ohio, who were the wives and daughters of the founders of the State, who shared equally in all the sacrifices then made.

Each applicant, when admitted deposits one hundred dollars, which is held as a reserve fund; this throws off the stigma of entire dependence. After this there is nothing more required of the inmates, except to live peaceably and in accordance with simple rules as regards a special care for general health.

Persons who pay twenty-five dollars are entitled to life membership. There are a number of these, and many who have given more. Through the Board of Managers and Mrs. Darby, the Matron, visitors and citizens are cordially invited to the Home, situated on Third street above Elevated Square, northern city limits.

The Board of lady Managers are:
    Mrs. W. L. Rolston, President.
    Mrs. George Irish, Vice President.
    Mrs. F. L. Ramsey, Secretary.
    Mrs. S. A. Eells, Treasurer.
    Mrs. T. D. Dale, Corresponding Secretary.

THE CHILDREN'S HOME.

One mile north of Marietta, near the banks of the Muskingum, is the first Home established, by legislative act of the State, for abandoned and orphaned children. Miss Catherine E. Fay, now Mrs. Ewing, of this city, first conceived the idea of a home for destitute children, rather than have them sent to the Infirmary.

She gathered a few waifs under her own roof, and cared for them, with the aid of charitable people, who interested themselves in the success of her mission. When her struggle to support and maintain them was more clearly brought to the attention of citizens, their sympathy was aroused, and a bill was introduced into the Legislature, and passed, for the establishment of this Home, to be supported by taxation. It has been in successful operation for twenty years; with the exception of a few years, under the charge of Dr. Simeon D. Hart, the Superintendent, and Miss Nixon, Matron, she succeeding Mrs. Hart after the death of this estimable lady a few years since.

There is now an average of over one hundred children, ranging in age from a few months to sixteen years. The property is valued at about forty thousand dollars. It is supported by direct taxation and the income from the farm. In this as in many other good works, this county was the first to inaugurate this method of caring for destitute children; the State came to its assistance in time of need. This Home has been a model, from which many counties of the state have established similar institutions.

One feature is to secure homes for the children in families before they arrive at the age of sixteen years, when they are dismissed from the care of the Home. The training and influence received, is scattered abroad where they are growing into manhood and womanhood as good citizens, ever thankful for the rescue there was in store for them.

MRS. LYDIA HART, who was Matron of this institution from 1869 to 1884, exerted a kind and motherly influence, and a devotion towards the children, seldom manifested as strongly as in her guidance and care for them. This was clearly significant at her death, when the heartfelt sorrow of the many motherless children showed their strong attachment for her. The loss was deeply felt by children and friends alike.

Churches.

In one of the block-houses, in Campus Martius, Rev. William Breck delivered the first sermon in the Northwest Territory. Rev. Manasseh Cutler preached a number of times during the summer of this first year of the settlement, while on a visit here. In 1789, Rev. Daniel Story was permanently employed by the settlers as their minister. He was preaching at Worcester, Massachusetts, but accepted the call to Marietta. He was the only ordained minister in the whole territory for a number of years, preaching at Waterford, Belpre, and in Virginia, besides his regular work here. He was installed as pastor of the first Congregational church of Marietta in 1788, so this church has a centennial of its organization, being the first church of the territory, and with a continued existence of one hundred years. Mr. Story died in December, 1804, and is buried in Mound Cemetery.

In Dr. Hildreth's History is found the following in regard to this Christian gentleman and minister of the Gospel: " In coming to Marietta, then a wilderness, he sacrificed his own interest, and his comfort, but knowing the necessities of the people, he was willing to part with many things for their good, and the cause of the Divine Master. What little wealth he possessed was invested in new lands before coming out, with an expectation of a reasonable support from the Ohio Company, until the rents of the lands set apart for the support of the Gospel should be available; but this was prevented by the Indian war, and no money was raised from that source until the year 1800. The inhabitants were generally much impovished from the same cause, and most probably his receipts from 1789 to 1797, could not have paid for his board and clothing. At his death the proceeds from the sale of his lands were insufficient to discharge the debts incurred while laboring in the new settlements, so that like a faithful servant he spent not only his life, but all his substance, in the service of the cause to which he was devoted." In the year 1796 he united and established the Fisst Congregational Society.

The First Religious Society was connected with the Congregational church, and after the Muskingum Academy was erected, worshipped in that building until the completion of the present church in 1809. This church was built under the management of its pastor, Rev. Samuel P. Robbins. The Methodist church was established in 1812.

A majority of all religious denominations is now here represented, and Marietta is often designated as the city of churches. It is remarkable in what close proximity the churches and school houses are found throughout this section, and all through the land. The first Sabbath schools and day schools were established in the block-houses surrounded by stockades, and these, it might be added, surrounded by Indians, and they so treacherous, that it could scarcely be determined when to trust them. The outgrowth of these pioneer schools has increased almost beyond comprehension. The next move towards better instruction and for the entertainment of the settlers was the establishment of libraries. There was an excellent one at Belpre with few, but instructive volumes as early as 1795, also one at Amestown in 1804. The first purchase of books for this library being an exchange of the pelts of the wild animals of the forest for books in Boston, which were brought to their destination with much difficulty.

Blennerhassett brought many books and other appliances for instruction, when he came and settled on the island bearing his name.

From what may seem these small beginnings have grown a State, and group of States noted for their thorough systems of education, and attention given to educational interests. This county does not lag in its training of the youth, and compares favorably with any in the State.

Table of Contents.

The First Settlement, Marietta,	9
The Ordinance of 1787,	17
The Mayflower,	21
State of Ohio Founded,	23
War with the Indians,	24
Defenses of the Frontiers,	29
Territorial Government,	38
Washington County,	39
Marietta,	41
The Ohio River,	43
Mills,	46
The Blennerhassetts,	49
Isaac and Rebecca Williams,	59
Two of Ohio's Governors,	62
Pioneer Association,	64
Marietta College,	77
Marietta Observatory,	80
Newspapers,	81
Harmar Cemetery,	82
Mound Cemetery,	83
Woman's Home,	94
Children's Home,	197
Churches,	99

Post Office—Front street, Railroad crossing.
Putnam Light Artillery—Headquarters at the Armory.
Rose Hill Sanitarium—Ten miles up the Ohio in West Virginia.
Riverside Fire Company—City Hall.
Soldiers' Monument—City Park.
Telegraph Office—Front street.
Telephone Office—Front Street, Register Building.
Woman's Home—Third street, above elevated square.
Woman's Relief Corps—Church street, Harmar, also corner Putnam and Second streets, Marietta.

CHURCH DIRECTORY, 1887.
MARIETTA.

First Congregational Church, Front street above Putnam, Rev. C. E. Dickinson, Pastor. Services 10½ A. M. and 7 P. M.; Sabbath School, 9½ A. M. Howard Stanley, Superintendent.

First Baptist Church, Putnam street above Third, Rev. Geo. R. Gear, Pastor. Services 10½ A. M. and 7 P. M.; Sabbath School 9 A. M. Chas. H. Turner, Supt.

First Unitarian Church, corner Putnam and Third streets. Rev. J. T. Lusk, Pastor. Services 10½ A. M. and 7 P. M.; Sabbath School 9 A. M. Jewett Palmer, Supt.

Fourth Street Presbyterian Church, Fourth street near Wooster, Rev. Wm. Addy, Pastor. Services 10½ A. M. and 7 P. M.; Sabbath School, 9 A. M. H. B. Shipman, Superintendent.

St. Luke's Episcopal Church, Second street above Putnam. Rector, Rev. John Boyd, D. D. Morning Prayer, 10½ A. M.; Evening Prayer, 7 P. M.; Sunday School, Edward F. Wells, Superintendent.

United Brethren Church, corner Second and Butler, Rev. M. E. Oliver, Pastor. Services 10½ A. M. and 7 P. M.; Sabbath School 9 A. M. James Patton, Supt.

German M. E. Church, corner Third and Wooster, Rev. Gustav H. Fiedler, Pastor. Services at 10½ A. M. and 7 P. M. Sabbath School 2 P. M. John Strecker, Jr., Superintendent.

St. Paul's German Evangelical Church, corner Fifth and Scammel, Rev. ———————, Pastor. Regular services 10½ A. M. and 7 P. M.; Sabbath School 2 P. M. Jacob Ebinger, Superintendent.

Methodist Episcopal Church, corner Wooster and Third streets, Rev. T. R. Taylor, Pastor. Regular services 10½ A. M. and 7 P. M.; Sabbath School, 9 A. M. Wesley G. Barthalow, Superintencent.

Wesleyan Methodist Church, Second street above Sacra Via. Rev. H. C. Pierce, Pastor. Sunday School at 3 P. M.

St. Lucas German Evangelical Church, corner Fourth and Scammel, Rev. Mr. Fleischer, Pastor. Regular service 10½ A. M.

African M. E. Church, Third street below Greene, Elder Davidson, Pastor. Regular services 10½ A. M. and 7 P. M.; Sabbath School, 3 P. M.

HARMAR.

First Congregational Church, corner Church and Second streets, Rev. H. C. Haskell, Pastor. Regular services 10½ A. M. and 7 P. M.; Sabbath School, 2 P. M. Romayne B. Hart, Superintendent.

Crawford M. E. Church, Rev. C. B. Longman, Pastor. Regular services 10½ A. M. and 7 P. M; Sabbath School, 2 P. M. John N. Price, Superintendent.

RAILROADS.

CINCINNATI, WASHINGTON & BALTIMORE.

Branch extension from Parkersburg to Marietta twelve miles from main line, connecting with lines East and West at Parkersburg.

For further information and the best possible rates, apply to Agent C., W. & B. Railroad, Marietta, Ohio, or to E. E. Patton, Traveling Passenger Agent, Chillcothe, O.

J. H. STEWART, Gen. Manager.   W. H. KING, Assistant G. P. A.

CLEVEAND & MARIETTA RAILWAY.

Through line between the Ohio and the Lakes, and all points in the Northwest, connecting with all points East and West, via the B. & O. at Cambridge, O., and the Pittsburg, Ft. Wayne & Chicago at Newcomerstown, O.

Connections made with all lines at junction points for all important cities East or West.   A. T. WIKOFF, President and General Manager.

F. G. JEWETT, General Passenger Agent.

For routes, rates, maps and full information call on or apply to

W. R. GRIMES, Agent, Marietta, Ohio.

MARIETTA, COLUMBUS & NORTHERN.

Connections.--At Moore's Junction with C., W. & B. Railway Co., at Marietta with C., W. & B. Railway Co., Wheeling & Lake Erie and Cleveland & Marietta Railways, Ohio River Railway, and with Passenger Packets on the Ohio and Muskingum rivers. For rates of freight or tickets apply at the General Office, Marietta, Ohio, or to   H. C. VINCENT, Freight and Passenger Agent.

R. E. PHILLIPS, Vice President and General Manager.

COLUMBUS, HOCKING VALLEY AND TOLEDO.

Direct connections made in Union Depot at Columbus, for Marietta, Pittsburg, Wheeling, Baltimore, Washington and Philadelphia; also for Dayton, Cincinnati, Louisville, and all points South and Southwest. Close connections at Toledo for Detroit and all points in Michigan and Canada.

H. J. FALKENBACH, General Passenger and Ticket Agent, Columbus, O.
G. R. CARR, General Superintendent.

OHIO RIVER RAILROAD.

Wheeling, Parkersburg, Point Pleasant, West Virginia. Connects at Wheeling with all routes East; also with Grafton, on the Baltimore & Ohio. The final terminus of the road is Huntington, W. Va., where it will connect with the Chesapeake & Ohio for Charleston, W. Va., and points South. Station for Marietta, Williamstown, W. Va. W. J. ROBINSON, General Passenger Agent.

CHARLES L. WILLIAMS, Assistant Superintendent, Parkersburg, W. Va.

A number of boats leave the wharves of Harmar and Marietta every day, and arrangements can be made with any of these railroads to take excursions to any point, up or down the Ohio, or up the Muskingum and return.

www.ingramcontent.com/pod-product-compliance
Lightning Source LLC
Chambersburg PA
CBHW031412160426
43196CB00007B/985